SUPERBOSS 2

To my late father
George Harold Freemantle
who was a Superboss without realising it

SUPER BOSS 2

THE NEW A-Z OF MANAGING PEOPLE SUCCESSFULLY

INTERNATIONAL SUPERSELLER

DAVID FREEMANTLE

Gower

First edition published 1985
by Gower Publishing Company Limited as *Superboss*

This edition published by
Gower Publishing Limited
Gower House
Croft Road
Aldershot
Hampshire GU11 3HR
England

Gower
Old Post Road
Brookfield
Vermont 05036
USA

David Freemantle has asserted his right under the Copyright, Designs and Patents Act 1988 to be identified as the author of this work.

British Library Cataloguing in Publication Data
Freemantle, David, 1942–
   Superboss 2: the new A–Z of managing people successfully
   1. Personnel management
   I. Title
   658.3

ISBN 0 566 07811 2

Library of Congress Cataloging-in-Publication Data
Freemantle, David.
   Superboss 2: the new A–Z of managing people successfully / David Freemantle.
      p.   cm.
   ISBN 0 566 07811 2 (cloth)
   1. Supervision of employees.   I. Title
   HF5549.12.F74   1997
   658.3—dc20   96–43274
                                                                                  CIP

Typeset in Great Britain by Intype London Ltd
and printed in Great Britain by Biddles Ltd, Guildford.

Contents

Preface

When *Superboss* was first published twelve years ago it represented a 'watershed' in my life. It was both an end and a beginning. I was forty-two, half way through my life and I had just ended twenty years developing my management career with a variety of 'blue-chip' companies which had culminated with a position on the board of a leading airline.

I had achieved much but was still frustrated that many of my ambitions remained unfulfilled: ambitions such as becoming a writer and running my own business. So, on leaving the airline, I decided to make a new beginning. *Superboss* became the focus for this. In the space of a couple of nights I drafted a proposal for the book and sent it off to four publishers. Amazingly two came back within seven days with offers of publication. This was the trigger, not only to complete the book but to set up my own consultancy company – which I also decided to name 'Superboss'.

I had always been a keen student of success, especially in the area of managing people, and during the previous twenty years I had formulated some very strong views about what makes a great boss. Many of these views were contrary to the current orthodoxy that you needed sophisticated management techniques (such as management by objectives, performance appraisal, briefing groups, quality circles etc.) to manage people effectively.

From the many managers I had met and closely observed I had concluded that the most successful were endowed with a healthy dose of common sense and a range of other basic qualities that bore little relation to the pseudo-scientific and jargonistic systems that the gurus were persuading companies to introduce.

In *Superboss* I attempted to reflect the common sense lessons that I had learnt over twenty years as well as give some simple guidance on the steps managers needed to take to become excellent bosses. I also tried to apply these lessons in the increasing volume of consultancy work I was undertaking for a wide variety of organisations around the world. My aim was (and is) to stimulate managers to become even more successful by moving away from these new-fangled convoluted bureaucratic practices and getting back to the basic essentials for motivating people and achieving great results.

In the years that have passed, the Superboss approach has become well established in many organisations. Furthermore the book has become immensely popular and has been translated into many languages, including most of the main European languages and also Indonesian and Chinese.

During these years I have gone on to write another five books all of which have had a measure of success, my subject range extending to customer service and business planning.

It came as no surprise therefore when Gower, my original publisher, invited me to produce a second edition of *Superboss*. I was delighted to agree but then found myself struggling to undertake the rewrite. I soon realised that I was in danger of rewriting many chapters just for the sake of rewriting. I had not read *Superboss* for some years and on re-reading I was reassured to find that the majority of topics covered are as relevant today as they were 12 years ago. The book has (and was intended to have) a certain timeless quality. To that extent it was difficult to update. Even so my thinking has moved on a little and I have, I believe, improved my writing style. The bulk of the changes in this new edition therefore take the form of amendments to existing sections. In some cases there has been a substantial rewrite of the section although in others just a sentence or a word has changed and there are twelve completely new sections whilst a similar number have been deleted.

My objective remains unchanged – to stimulate and challenge the reader to examine his or her personal behaviours with a view to developing practices which will ensure that everyone around describes him, or her, as a Superboss!

I would welcome readers' comments and would urge them to contact me at:

Superboss Ltd

Tel: +44(0)1753 833226
Fax: +44(0)1753 863412
e-mail: team@superboss.co.uk
web-site: http:/www.superboss.co.uk

David Freemantle

Acknowledgements

The book *Superboss* has been around for over ten years now. I would like to thank Malcolm Stern at Gower who supported the book from the very beginning and who subsequently encouraged me to write *Superboss 2*.

I would also like to thank my wife Mechi for her loyal support over this period of time and for her contribution, as an expert proofreader, in ensuring the high quality of the finished typescript.

DF

Introduction

You too can be a Superboss. Once you've dipped into this book you'll probably realise you're almost one already.

Many people have made a lot of money over the last thirty years or so developing and expounding the idea that to be an effective manager you need to pass psychometric tests, go through assessment centres, attend high-level management training courses and business schools and, what is worse, even read books on management!

Furthermore over the same period a myth has been perpetrated by the so-called personnel professionals that the management of people is an incredibly complicated science.

But the Superboss doesn't let this stand in the way of managing people successfully. He doesn't hide behind excuses such as the lack of clear direction from the company. You will never hear the Superboss saying, for example: 'How can I do a good management job? This company doesn't know where it is going, it doesn't invest in training, and employee relations issues are always dealt with up in Personnel.'

The Superboss knows what he has to achieve and sets out to achieve it, overcoming any obstacles put in his way. The Superboss knows how to encourage his people to support him, irrespective of whether the Chief Executive is crazy, the Vice-President Finance incompetent, or his immediate boss plain bloody ignorant.

The Superboss doesn't spend his time looking for excuses. He puts up with all the inadequacies of his highly imperfect company and buckles down and does a good job, taking his people with him.

The Superboss has learnt a great deal about people. For a start he knows that his own boss is far from perfect and therefore needs a lot of help. He has learnt about how people behave, what they respect, what they want. He hasn't learnt this by going to school, but by continually questioning his own experience, learning from his own mistakes.

The Superboss has learnt that the main determinant in motivating his people is his own relationship with them. As a result he invests a substantial proportion of his time in developing these relationships. He knows that his staff will judge him by every word he says, every memo he writes, every action he takes and every decision he makes.

He knows that he needs to be totally consistent in his approach. In fact he knows that it is his behaviour, his attitudes, his decisions which will make or break his team – not the behaviour, attitudes and decisions of senior executives, nor the behaviour, attitudes and decisions of union officials or those of the Personnel Department or Finance.

The Superboss knows that the prime factor in his team's motivation and performance is himself, the boss. He will achieve in any circumstances. Over a period of time, the Superboss has developed an extensive range of successful management practices which he knows will lead to maximum team motivation and performance. These do not derive from employee relations strategies, personnel policies or directives handed down from above. They relate to what a Superboss does, minute by minute, hour by hour, to maintain and develop the motivation and performance of his total team.

More often than not these management practices are straightforward common sense, a fact often obscured by writers and lecturers on management. Common sense has to be challenged however, otherwise it is in danger of becoming distorted sense.

This book sets out to challenge readers by presenting an 'A to Z' of common sense but essential practices for managing people successfully, an 'A to Z' of what a manager should actually do to become a Superboss.

The Superboss can be the Chief Executive of an airline, the supervisor in charge of the switchboard or the Production Manager in Factory 2. The Superboss can be anyone responsible for supervising, managing or directing people, whether they number 10, 100 or 10,000.

And of course the Superboss can be male or female. In the text, for simplicity's sake, I have used 'he' and 'him' to stand for 'he or she' and 'him or her'.

This book is intended not to be read from cover to cover, but 'dipped into', perhaps on a page-a-day basis. It is meant to provide, for anyone concerned with managerial excellence, a guide to the action you as a manager can take today towards achieving this and becoming a Superboss.

Once you've dipped into the book a number of times it will be clear that underlying all the entries is a consistent philosophy of what constitutes successful people management.

As an aspiring Superboss don't wait for the company to enrol you on the next management training course. Start today by putting into practice what you read in this book.

It won't be long before you're a Superboss!

Superboss 2

The new A–Z of
managing people successfully

Accountability

Accountability is knowing what you'll be fired for

The Superboss goes out of his way to make sure he is 100 per cent clear about his accountabilities. He knows what decisions he can make, how to delegate accountability and how to encourage members of his team to make decisions.

Whoever makes a decision carries the buck – must be held accountable after the event. Which is why, in poorly-run companies, people try to pass the buck and why inefficient decision-stifling bureaucracies build up. In such companies issues requiring decisions eddy around in a swirling sea of bureaucracy, committees and upward delegation. The issue will eventually surface with some high-up person who will be forced to say yes or no and will then be criticised furiously behind his or her back for making the wrong decision. The critics will be the very same people who passed the buck in the first place.

The Superboss has nothing of this. He'll make a decision and carry the can. If he's unclear whether it's his decision or not he'll either check with his boss or preferably take a flyer and make the decision himself. The Superboss has learnt that the best way of clarifying grey accountability areas is to make decisions and wait until someone challenges him. That's his opportunity formally to clarify the accountability.

Of course, the Superboss knows that if he makes more than one bad decision he might be fired. Being accountable takes guts! But he never is fired. He's learnt that it's easier to get forgiveness for a bad decision than permission for a good one.

ACTION TODAY

Sit down today and clarify your own levels of accountability. Make sure you know what business decisions you can make. Better still, make a list of those unresolved issues and start making some decisions; you can account to your boss later. Discuss accountability with your team. Take them out for a drink after work and charge it to the company. See who challenges your decision and then account for that decision.

If you're dissatisfied that you can't authorise travel, recruitment, training and basic expenditure, go and discuss it with your boss and ensure you are fully clear about your accountabilities when you leave the meeting.

Confirm today that the company is holding you accountable for production levels, sales targets, engineering performance, distribution deadlines, cost-effective administration or whatever is your line of management.

You need to know today that you are being held accountable for the success of your department, or the failure. If you don't know the difference between success and failure in your area you should resign immediately – either you have an impossible job, or you are an impossible buck-passer.

It starts with you, find out! To be able to manage you must be accountable.

REMEMBER

You are a SUPERBOSS if you can make decisions and account for them.

Achievement

Achievement is what management is all about

It's horrifying to interview so many managers who are unable to summarise what they've achieved in their career to date. Some talk about promotion as an achievement. Yes, for them personally. But, I ask, what have they achieved for the company? Then many are lost. Some talk about their skills, or their hard work, or what they actually do, week by week.

Achievement is the bench-mark for the Superboss. It is what he has personally contributed, apart from every other manager, to the profitability and success of the company. It's the added value he brings to his customers through excellent service, it's the exceptionally high standards he consistently achieves. It's his track record and he's proud of it. His achievements are the total contribution he and his team bring to the bottom-line results of the company.

Those achievements, which he'll measure either quantitatively or qualitatively, might include the successful introduction of a new product, or efficiency improvements in the loading bay, or a one per cent reduction in labour turnover, or recruiting into the company some of the country's top graduates, or consistent on-time delivery for twelve months, or a reduction in the number of customer complaints from his predecessor's level, or saving the company considerable expenditure by improving the administration. It might be winning important new contracts against intensive competition, or increasing market share or the successful venture into new markets.

Whatever his achievements they are end results his people can relate to and his own bosses appreciate.

The Superboss knows that he must achieve to be of any value to the organisation. Even routine management functions present achievement opportunities for the Superboss – he will raise standards of housekeeping and output quality (whether that output be a car component or a response to a customer request).

ACTION TODAY

Draft out your career résumé including a summary of your greatest achievements over recent years. If you are unable to identify recent achievements you should be leaving the company before a Superboss catches up with you.

ACTION TOMORROW

What achievements do you plan over the next six months? If you have no such plan you will achieve nothing!

REMEMBER

Achievement differentiates the SUPERBOSS from the 'manager ordinaire'.

Action

Action is the language of commitment, it speaks louder than words

We've all experienced it. The situation where someone says something will be done and it isn't. The sales manager who promises to ring you but doesn't, the service manager who promises to order your parts and call you back but doesn't, the employee relations specialist who promises to send you a copy of the standard contract of employment, but doesn't.

There's the manager who is always telling you it's someone else's problem. 'I can't sort out the scheduling', the production manager will tell you, 'you'd better see planning'.

The Superboss will take action, he'll speak to the planning people on your behalf. If the Superboss says he'll arrange for a copy of the employment contract to be sent to you, he'll take action, it will be sent to you. If the Superboss promises to solve your parts problem he will.

When the Superboss decides to help you he's committing himself to take action. When you take a problem to him and ask for help he assumes that's what you want. He won't refer you to another manager. He won't shrug his shoulders and say 'What can I do?' He won't forget two minutes later what he said. He'll do something about your problem. He'll make a note of the agreed action, and then he'll do what he said he'd do.

If there's a problem his team are struggling with, he'll take action to help. He'll step in and ring the chief executive of Mossley's when his team are struggling to obtain supplies from them. He'll see the financial director when the purchasing manager receives continual complaints from Mossley's about excessive delays in payments.

When Lucy Wight asks for five minutes to complain that Personnel seems to be blocking her transfer, the Superboss will take immediate action and ring Personnel to find out why.

When his boss comes in and mentions that at a dinner last night the president of one of their main customers made some confused comment about service delays, the Superboss will take action. He'll examine the problem and have a report on his boss's desk before the day is out.

The Superboss will always take action.

ACTION TODAY

Take some positive action on every single problem that comes your way. Don't leave it till tomorrow, don't pass it up to your boss, don't leave it for one of your colleagues.

Take action to fix the problem, whatever it is. If you see the problem, it's your problem. So take action.

REMEMBER

You will always see a SUPERBOSS where the action is.

9

Advice

A manager cannot function effectively without advice

It's not easy to give advice, let alone take it. Some managers become defensive whenever you offer it. It's as if the process of accepting advice is a process of admitting your own ignorance, exposing your own inadequacies.

Other more assertive managers develop 'barriers against advice'. They assume an arrogant facade of a thousand answers, appearing to know everything. They will shake their head, frown and cut you short if you so much as dare to offer advice.

The managers who resist advice normally get their come-uppance when there's an organisation change, or a new boss comes in.

The Superboss will give advice, and he'll take it. If he's not in a position to give it, he'll advise where to go for it. His advice is always aimed at helping a person, whether it be to resolve a problem, or improve performance or whatever. In rendering advice his motives are always honourable, never Machiavellian nor political.

His advice is not always solicited. You might see the Superboss take Ben Giovanni by the elbow to give some gentle advice about not 'mouthing off' in front of others. Or when Neil Bloch comes up for a signature the Superboss will seize the opportunity to seek Neil's advice on the problems with delays in despatch.

The Superboss is always prepared to be influenced by advice from his team, his boss, his colleagues. If the decision he has to make is not perfectly clear he'll seek advice: 'Now, Ben, perhaps you'll give *me* some advice. If you were in my shoes what would you do about this problem with allowances . . .?'

The Superboss recognises that he is not the sole custodian of expertise in his department. He likes to think he has helped develop the expertise of the people around him. Why squander that expertise? Take advice from the experts, that's what the Superboss does.

ACTION TODAY

Take advice. Spend your whole day seeking advice from people around you about the problems facing the company, the department and them. Listen carefully and don't shoot them down if they make crazy suggestions. You don't have to accept their advice, but try very hard to. After all, one or two of them might be in your shoes tomorrow, and even doing a better job than you.

REMEMBER

If you want to be a SUPERBOSS, take advice from one.

Aims

Without aims a manager will miss out on everything

The blind leading the blind. I've seen them stumbling along those long dark corridors of bureaucratic organisations – managers searching for decisions, managers acting as messenger boys between supervisors who need a decision and senior executives who make them.

These managers will tell you one day that cutting back on costs is the highest priority and the next day that it's investing in customer service. They change their priorities constantly. They thoroughly confuse their staff who end up working aimlessly in a bureaucracy of conflicting signals.

The Superboss selects his aim and maintains it. When the Superboss says 'Supervisory training has become our highest priority', you'll still hear him saying it in three or six months' time. Everyone will be clear about his aim.

The Superboss does not have all his people rushing blindly in different directions. He connects his aim to the profit, customer service and people objectives of the business; he ensures it's clear and focused and then communicates it to his people, following through to ensure everyone is moving in the same direction.

If the aim is a notable improvement in telephone handling standards, he'll clarify exactly what is required; he'll ensure that all his people are aware of it and push cohesively for that improvement. In six months' time when telephones at both the switchboard and the extension are consistently answered within five seconds and with a warm friendly response he might well change his aim, but until then that aim will be maintained and reinforced.

ACTION TODAY

What are your main aims over the next six months? Write them down. You should have no more than six. Three would be better.

How do these aims fit in to the overall aims of the company?

ACTION TOMORROW

Check with your team that they are 100 per cent clear about these aims.

ACTION NEXT WEEK

Take a stroll to the furthest corner of your organisation (even if it means stepping into an aeroplane), and check that the first person you meet there is clear about your aims, is pointing in the same direction and working towards that end. You might be surprised at the result.

ACTION NEXT MONTH

Maintain these aims and reinforce them.

REMEMBER

A SUPERBOSS always aims high.

Appraisal

Appraisal should be an integral part of everyday management, not a centralised bureaucratic system imposed on unwilling managers

Whoever invented the appraisal form should be jailed. (No wonder he or she remains anonymous.)

Appraisal forms have kept whole personnel empires going for many decades and created a pseudo-science of performance ratings and analysis. Life wouldn't be the same for many personnel people if they couldn't thrust a blank appraisal form in the face of a busy manager.

This is no excuse for not appraising people. Appraisal is absolutely essential but you don't really need a form to do it. If it helps, fine – use two sheets of lined plain paper.

To the Superboss appraisal is second nature. He does it informally on a daily basis as an integral part of his task of managing people. Once or twice a year he'll appraise his team members more formally by sitting down with each of them and reviewing what they've achieved. He'll encourage them to appraise themselves against the objectives and standards formerly agreed. Furthermore they'll discuss areas for improvement including those in which he can help. Appraisal must be a two-way process.

The Superboss knows that if you require a certain performance level and contribution from an individual, then you must give that individual feedback on whether or not it's being achieved. That's appraisal, that's management.

The Superboss never links appraisal to the assessment of pay. He knows that if pay is directly linked to appraisal an individual will naturally become defensive, will want to cover up weaknesses (which the Superboss could well help with) and exaggerate strengths.

Therefore, the last thing the Superboss will want is an appraisal system in which he has to rate each manager out of 10. Performance rating in this manner tends to be subjective, demotivational and, to be honest, pseudo-scientific and irrelevant. Appraisal should be a positive, constructive method of helping an individual do better. It is essentially a development process.

ACTION TODAY

Check your diary and make sure you have appraisals scheduled for each member of your team over the next twelve months. If you haven't appraised a member of your team within the last twelve months arrange to do so immediately. Keep a record of the appraisal if you think that helps, but remember, appraisals are not witch hunts, nor insurance records, nor pay determinants.

REMEMBER

The first person to be appraised is always the SUPERBOSS.

Assessment

You can assess a manager by assessing his or her people

Assessment is relating a person to the job. It is a process of clarifying what the job entails, specifying the type of person best suited to that job and making a careful and objective judgement about the person under consideration.

The Superboss devotes considerable time to assessing people, not only for a job, but in the job. The Superboss knows that if he gets the assessment process wrong he cannot succeed. To rush assessment and devote insufficient time to it is to put at peril your company and its people.

The Superboss's assessment is always objective. If a job becomes vacant he'll first assess whether or not the job is needed. Sometimes he'll surprise himself and find that the job can be abolished – other people can cover the task involved. Having confirmed the job, he'll assess very carefully what it entails in terms of duties, responsibilities and results to be achieved. He'll also assess the skills, attributes and experience requirements for the ideal candidate. Finally he'll carefully interview the candidates, obtaining as much information about them as possible in relation to their own skills, attributes and experience.

He will always involve other people in the assessment process knowing that this will help with a wide range of useful insights. However, the final decision will always be his, because only he will be accountable for managing the successful candidate's performance. Once the candidate is in the job the Superboss will assess the new recruit's performance on a continuous basis with a view to identifying ways the person can further develop on the job.

The assessment process is critical for the Superboss. He knows that the best results can only be achieved by a rigorously systematic and objective approach although it does not have to be bureaucratic. His whole team is in fact a reflection of his assessment capability.

ACTION TODAY

Critically review the way you assess people, not only recruitment or promotion candidates, but also your existing people. Do you devote enough time to this critical task? Do you always co-operate with Personnel when they try to help you specify what is required? Do you opt out and leave the task to Personnel?

Identify at least two ways in which you can improve your approach to assessment. It will be reflected in your results.

Furthermore, assess the potential of your people to develop in the job and eventually for more responsible positions elsewhere.

REMEMBER

The SUPERBOSS is always assessing himself and seeks help from his people for that purpose.

Awareness

You can't solve problems unless you are aware of them. Many managers are so unaware of problems they get blown up by them

It's called the ivory tower syndrome. In some organisations they might refer to the 'seventh floor' or 'Head Office' in the same way.

It's managers who divorce themselves from reality by spending 80 per cent of their time in their offices, reading memos and reports, making telephone calls, receiving them, and attending countless meetings. Somewhere outside is a real world, but they are not aware of it. A real world in their own company. Real people who have real problems. That reality cannot be brought to life by reading reports or attending meetings.

The Superboss is fully aware of events around him. To become aware he doesn't rely on the communications that arrive at his office, nor on the people who knock at his door. The Superboss goes out and about, sees and hears for himself. Occasionally he even joins the front-line team and works with them for a day. Problems take on a different perspective that way. When people tell him they're having difficulty over at Greenyard with the new filtration system the Superboss goes over there and sees for himself. He gains a new perspective – they weren't just moaning as usual about new equipment, but do seem to have a genuine and repetitive flow restriction problem.

By being fully aware the Superboss is in the best position to help and lend support.

But it's not only awareness of physical problems, it's awareness of the employee relations climate too. The Superboss is aware of his people's feelings, of their concerns and grievances. He moves around, chats to them, listens, becomes aware of what they're thinking. This helps him nip problems in the bud, helps him address issues before they grow into something bigger.

In determing what his people really feel he never puts them down or dismisses their comments should they be critical of his own approach and hurtful. In becoming aware, the Superboss is first and foremost aware of what people truly think and feel about him.

ACTION TODAY

Carry out a team awareness test. Gather your immediate team together and, using a whiteboard or flip-chart, ask each person to state what they believe is the biggest problem facing their people today. You should contribute to this part of the test by adding what you believe it is.

ACTION TOMORROW

Spend twenty minutes walking around each section with the member of your team responsible. Stop and talk to every other person. For example: 'Say Suzy, if you were to tell me the biggest problem facing you here at work what would it be?' Make a quick note of what Suzy says, and then what Maria, José, Jack, Mazie and Pedro say also.

ACTION THE DAY AFTER TOMORROW

Collect your team together and present a collation of your findings. Compare them with the original list. What does the awareness test show?

ACTION NEXT MONTH

Find out what your team really think and feel about you!

REMEMBER

The SUPERBOSS never forgets that his people need to be aware too (of what's going on and what he thinks).

Behaviour

It is the fine behaviours of managers that determines their success or otherwise in motivating people to deliver high performance

A boss's behaviour is observed every minute of the working day (and often beyond). It forms the basis upon which people all around judge a person in authority.

Behaviour includes the clothes the boss wears and how they are worn. It includes the state of the hair and fingernails. It includes every single word the boss utters and whether or not he or she uses Lagerfield cologne or suffers from body odour. It includes the state of the office and how the boss answers the phone. (You can tell a lot by whether the response is: 'Jackie Jones here', or '2348' or 'Jones'!) It includes whether the door is open and the boss is always available, or whether the door is shut and the boss is too busy. It includes the extent to which the boss uses common courtesies (like opening doors for everyone, whether they be front-line people, visitors or senior executives).

Behaviour is everything a boss does. It forms the basis for this book. Achievement stems from behaviour.

The Superboss is completely conscious of and in command of his behaviour. He sets the highest standards of behaviour in every respect, ranging from the way he greets visitors to the building to the way he helps people with problems. He doesn't scowl at the apologetic clerk forcing his way through the door for an urgent signature, nor does he continually look at his watch when the Employee Relations manager prattles on. The Superboss never fiddles expenses nor gets drunk on formal occasions. He might tell jokes, but they are never offensive. His behaviour commands respect, underpins his authority.

The Superboss, even so, knows that he is not perfect, that his behaviour cannot always be immaculate. But he always tries to conform to the highest standards, and expects his team to do the same.

ACTION TODAY

Watch your behaviour – every minute of the day. Try to be conscious of every eye movement you make when you're with people. Try to control your tendency to sigh, scratch your ear, shake your head, look out of the window. If you want to communicate something to a person, be direct and be polite. It's better to interrupt and say 'I'm going to have to close this meeting in five minutes', rather than continually glance at your watch.

Furthermore try to make your behaviour 'pro-active' as opposed to 'reactive'.

Starting today, discipline yourself to be totally conscious of and in command of your behaviour at all times.

REMEMBER

There can be no higher standard of behaviour in an organisation than that set by a SUPERBOSS.

Beliefs

To be a successful manager you must have a set of personal beliefs which you can put into practise every day

Beliefs should form the basis of everything you do as a manager. Without beliefs you will blow with the wind, become reactive.

It is your beliefs which should guide your everyday behaviour as well as your longer-term strategic action.

If you believe something is important you will do it. If you believe it is important to listen carefully to what your people say and take the appropriate action then you will do it. If you believe it is important to pay your people well to achieve the best results then you will do it. If you believe it is important to invest in training then you will do it.

However if your beliefs are weak or non-existent then your behaviours, actions and decisions will be driven by people with stronger beliefs.

A careful study of the most successful managers will reveal that they all have a strong set of beliefs. This doesn't mean that you have to agree with all these beliefs. The real test for the Superboss is what do to when you are faced with a group of people with different beliefs on what is important and how to proceed.

In this case the Superboss will accept the difference and believe the decision should be made by the person accountable for delivering the result. It might be, regrettably, that not everyone believes this decision is right.

The Superboss will have developed his beliefs over a long career at work. He will challenge other people's beliefs (for example the belief that the 'carrot and stick' approach to management is effective) as well as encourage others to challenge his beliefs.

ACTION TODAY

Quickly scan some other sections in this book. You will sense a set of underlying management beliefs which the Superboss will have. Do they accord with your own beliefs?

Take one or two of your colleagues for a drink after work today and debate the issue with them. It is of vital importance to you. You must have an effective framework of management beliefs. What are they?

REMEMBER

It is the beliefs of a SUPERBOSS which form the basis of every-thing he does.

Believe

Believing in yourself and your people is the essence of success in management

Seeing is believing, or so it is said.

The Superboss sees his people working hard, sees them achieving results, sees them putting themselves out.

The Superboss believes in his people because he believes they will do their best for the company, for the department, and for him as well as themselves. They do their best for him because they believe in him, because they believe he will do his best for them.

The Superboss believes in his people because he is proud of them, proud of what they've achieved already, the effort they've put in and what they'll achieve in the future.

The Superboss shows he believes in them by reflecting what he sees, letting them know he's seen them working hard, achieving results, putting themselves out.

And when his people perform badly, or make mistakes he pats them on the back and tells them that he himself is always making mistakes and could do better, that he has made a thousand mistakes in his time. He tells them he still believes in them.

The Superboss believes in his people because he believes in himself. He sees all their weaknesses in himself, as well as their strengths. He believes, in fact knows, that he is forever doing his best. He believes, in fact knows, that his people are also doing their best. If not he would immediately confront the issue. No one will ever admit to not doing their best. If perceptions of 'the best' vary, the Superboss will explore the variation with the individual or people concerned.

ACTION TODAY

Ask yourself, 'Do my people believe in me?' If you don't know the answer, they probably don't. It's probably because you don't believe in them.

Ask yourself, 'Do I believe in every member of my team?'

If not, and there's a person you don't believe in, you have a serious problem. Consult your closest confidant and then call up the person and confront the issue, exploring why you don't think you believe in him or her (i.e. why you don't believe he or she is giving of his or her best). Don't accuse, just discreetly explore the problem. There's no other way you can work.

REMEMBER

The SUPERBOSS believes in himself and his people.

Bottom line

Ultimately it is the bottom line that should determine everything you do

In a capitalist society there is no denying the ultimate goal of profit. However, to exploit people to arrive at profit is anathema to the Superboss.

There are two distinctly opposing views on how people should relate to profit and the Superboss subscribes to only one of them.

The first is to view people as a cost which has a direct impact on the profit and loss account. In other words to enhance profit you have to reduce costs. As people are a major part of your costs you have to minimise their numbers and their pay.

The second is to view people as an asset which has a direct impact on the balance sheet. In other words to enhance your long term profitability and dividends you have to invest in people.

The Superboss subscribes to the latter view. He believes his people are an asset which adds value to the business. He therefore invests resources to ensure that the very best people are recruited to the business, that they are paid well and also trained and developed to the highest standards of performance. He also invests a substantial part of his time daily to ensure effective two-way communication with his people and to secure their continued motivation.

However, in doing all this his long-term aim is to secure the required bottom-line results for his company and therefore to secure the jobs of the people working for it.

All his efforts therefore are directed towards this bottom-line result. He only sanctions expenditure which he believes will contribute, directly or indirectly, to profitability.

He is conscious all the time of the impact his decisions and the efforts of his team will have on the bottom line of the company. He does not believe screwing his people down on pay or numbers will serve that result.

ACTION TODAY

Sit down over lunch with some of your people and try to relate what you do to the bottom line of the company. In what way do you and your people add value to the profitability (short-term or long-term) of the company?

The simple test is to ask yourself, 'What would be the negative impact on the company's results if they eliminated my job and those of my people?' If you cannot answer this, then your job deserves to be eliminated!

REMEMBER

The SUPERBOSS profits by putting people before profit.

Bouncing back

Success is synonymous with failure from which all successful people bounce back

The route to success is never a straight line. It is littered with obstacles, pot-holes, hurdles, diversions and barriers. Even the most successful people stumble at times.

They make mistakes, they choose unwisely and they despair that they are ever going to achieve success.

The Superboss knows that when the going is good it is easy to be positive. The trick is to be positive when the going is bad, when orders have been lost, when profitability is low, when the contracts do not come in, when customers defect, when productivity slips, when key people leave, when quality is in decline, when recessions set in, when markets decline, when competitors leap ahead and when the new Chief Executive threatens dire consequences.

The Superboss takes his energy from his studies of successful people such as Nelson Mandela, Tina Turner and Jung Chang. He is inspired by their stories of adversity and bouncing back. He knows that the setbacks they experienced were a thousand times worse than he'll ever experience.

So when things go wrong for a Superboss he reminds himself of these successful people. There is always light at the end of the tunnel.

ACTION TODAY

Initiate a study of adversity and of successful people who have overcome it. This will help you to be well prepared for those disastrous
days which we all experience.

REMEMBER

When others have given up, the SUPERBOSS always bounces
back.

Briefing

Be briefed, brief and be brief about it

The principle behind briefing groups is great.

The danger is that they become just another bureaucratic system substituted for a key management task. Managers will no longer see their task as briefing people, but to issue company briefings.

There is a risk that briefings are used for propaganda purpose, to convey messages down the line and to exhort or brainwash people into thinking differently. There are stories of briefings being invariably full of 'gloom and doom' (the Vice President of Finance making the point that every time we raise expectations with good news 'they' will expect a pay increase).

There are other stories of managers pinning briefings on notice-boards and then popping their heads around the rest room door to scatter a few more copies on the table for the 'workers' to read. That was it. That was the briefing.

The Superboss makes a point first of keeping himself briefed all the time, and then of ensuring that his people are briefed as soon as possible. If the company produces a written briefing, fine, he'll use it to supplement his own briefing. The Superboss knows what interests his people and he briefs them on those subjects. He encourages questions after the briefing and if he doesn't know an answer he'll go and find it. Although the company briefing might refer to an exceptional provision this month for exchange losses, the Superboss will know that his people would prefer to be briefed on when the new fork lift trucks are going to be delivered, or when the company is going to renovate their rest room, or when the new warehousing procedure is due to start.

The Superboss keeps his briefings brief. They are always relevant, always face to face, always frequent and he always provides sufficient time for questions. The Superboss briefs on a regular (even daily) basis and calls impromptu briefing sessions when necessary.

ACTION TODAY

If you haven't briefed your people personally within the last month you should be fired immediately.

Check your diary and allocate sufficient time for briefing sessions over the next four weeks. These should be big priority. Prepare your own briefing carefully, using the most recent company briefing, but concentrating on issues that will interest your people. Allocate sufficient time for questions. Don't just brief your immediate reports, go along and contribute to their briefing sessions down the line.

REMEMBER

With his briefings the SUPERBOSS beats the grapevine every time.

Caring

Care for your people, then they'll care for you and the company

Don't simulate care. If you can't be bothered with your people, don't bother.

The personnel policy for the organisation might be 'We want to be a people-caring employer', but that means nothing unless every supervisor, manager and director cares for his or her staff.

The Superboss cares for his people, tries hard to help them with their problems. Furthermore he shows he cares, shows he's interested in their successes, concerned about their failures. He takes care about their training, development and career procession. He's careful to give advice and counsel when it's needed. He always takes care to be available.

When things go wrong at home, the Superboss cares enough to see if he can help in any way. He's discreet, but interested. He gives his people time off when they have personal problems and often before they ask.

If anyone is ill he will send a card, some flowers, some magazines – even a bottle of whisky. His concern is always genuine and he'll even break the rules to show it.

First and foremost however, the Superboss will always wander along to see someone with a problem and ask how things are. He cares that much.

His caring approach is reflected in everything he does, in every little behaviour, in the way he speaks to people.

The Superboss also genuinely cares for his customers. He cares that they receive the best, that their needs are met and their problems fixed. This means that he cares for high performance. What he does not care for is poor performance. But he deals with poor performance in a caring way.

ACTION TODAY

Commit yourself to taking at least one people-caring action today and every day. It doesn't take too much imagination. For example, find out who's absent sick and make some positive gesture such as sending a card. This is not a job for the welfare officer, it's a job for you the Superboss.

Or wander along to see anyone who has just returned to work after a period of illness and show some genuine concern for his or her welfare.

Take an interest today in your people and show you care. They should be very precious to you and you should be proud of them!

REMEMBER

If you care to be a SUPERBOSS, you must care.

Challenge

The worst managers manage the status quo, whilst the best create challenges which leave others behind

Climbing Everest, flying to the moon or writing million-seller books are no bigger challenges than that of motivating people to achieve phenomenal results. They are all in fact challenges of management. Nobody climbs Everest, reaches the moon, or has a book published without a well managed team to support him or her. The real challenge is to develop a successful approach to management which achieves the desired result.

The physical side (equipment etc.) is relatively easy. The challenge for the Superboss is twofold. Firstly, to identify opportunities which will put the company way ahead of the competition. Secondly, to apply his unique skills to develop a superb team to exploit that opportunity.

Challenges don't come every day and are never routine. It might be to introduce a new product on the market in super-quick time. It might be to retrieve an important customer who defected three years ago. It might be to tender for a leading public service organisation. Or it might be to hire the very best people in a tight competitive market place. It might just be to turn a company or department around from atrocious performance to excellence.

The Superboss loves challenges, seizes them like gold dust, uses them as chances to boost the motivation of his team, to set their adrenalin going, give them excitement. If it means working 18 hours without stopping, then he'll be there too – meeting the challenge with them working 18 hours without stopping.

The Superboss thrives on challenge, and so does his team. As a result the challenges tend to come his way. People seem to know.

ACTION TODAY

Call your team together and ask them what sort of challenges they really relish. Then ask what they see as the biggest challenge facing them over the coming months.

Agree with them on what challenges will set their adrenalin going and achieve maximum motivation.

REMINDER

You become a SUPERBOSS by rising to the challenge.

Change

Progress is synonymous with change

If nothing ever changes in an organisation then it becomes an exceedingly boring place. Its products become dowdy, its services dated, its environment dreary, its machinery dilapidated and its people deadly dull.

Dull and dreary people resist change. They feel secure in the comfort of what they already know. Change frightens them, whether it be a new computer system, a new boss or a new office to work in. They become fixed in rigid thinking patterns, not prepared to flex or try out new ideas.

The Superboss knows that there is no alternative to change. The environment is changing all the time (new technology, new markets, new governments, new attitudes) whilst the competition always seems to be racing ahead. There are always pressures for more efficient working practices, for new technology, for new products, for new sales campaigns and even for new people.

The Superboss thrives on change, loves it. It keeps his adrenalin going and gives him the satisfaction of learning new processes all the time, of adding value through constant improvement. But he recognises the fears his people have, the insecurity they feel. So he spends time with them, explaining and discussing the need for change, reassuring them, attempting to excite their interest. He persuades them that a change to a new electronic mail system is absolutely necessary; that pay anomalies are such that there is no option but to change to a new job evaluation system; that shortage of space means a move to a new office across the road. The Superboss persuades them that a change to reduced staffing levels must take place now that automated packaging has come in, reassuring them at the same time that natural wastage will take care of the reduction.

Whatever the change the Superboss takes care to do the right thing by his people, the best he can for them. He'll never rush change. He'll spend time consulting his people about it, attempting to take them along with him, explaining the benefits of the change, gaining their consent and co-operation.

The last thing a Superboss wants to do is impose change, but sometimes it is the last thing he has to do.

ACTION TODAY

Walk around your area and ask each person you meet: 'If there's one change you would like to see here, what would it be?' Review your findings with your immediate subordinates and draw up a plan to make the agreed changes. Then go back to the people who wanted the change and advise them of your plans.

REMEMBER

If there's nothing to change you don't need a SUPERBOSS.

Character

The character of the manager is reflected in the character of his or her team

Characterless is colourless. Characterless is having no personality, no life, no excitement, no interests, no energy.

There are characterless managers who tick over day by day, pushing papers around, waiting for problems to reach their desk and then deflecting them on to someone else. If such managers do have character it is but to moan and groan and criticise everyone else: their bosses, their colleagues and even their subordinates. Often their colourless character is reflected in their dull dress and two-dimensional expressionless personalities.

To be characterless as a manager is to be negative in the extreme.

The Superboss has character, is a character. His character shows in the way he deals with people, his boss, his staff, his colleagues. It shows in how he handles situations and the problems that come his way. It shows in the little eccentricities people love him for. His character gives colour to their everyday working lives.

The colour of the Superboss's character shows through. It bears a distinctive mark which people see and talk about. 'One thing you have to learn about the boss,' people will say to a new member of their team about their Superboss, 'is to keep out of his way when Liverpool have lost; that's the only time he'll ever snap at you. It always takes him two days to recover and if you want anything you'll have to wait until then.' Other people might tell you 'He's a great boss, but you won't know him until you've had your first bollocking. Be prepared for it, it will be some experience, but after that you'll have his total confidence and support.'

The character of the Superboss will be reflected in the character of his team because they will reflect his values and his beliefs. What is important for him will be important for them.

ACTION TODAY

Write this at the back of your diary: *'As from now I will never ever undertake any character assassination: boss, senior executive, chief executive, subordinate, colleague or acquaintance'*.

Then think about ways of developing your own character and the character of your team. To be a Superboss your character must have a positive distinctive mark. What is it?

Check on it. Take your personnel manager into your confidence and ask for help in giving some feedback on how people see your character.

REMEMBER

The SUPERBOSS characterises all that is best in the company.

Clarity

Would you drive a car without clear vision?

Autocratic managers are very bad at clarity – especially egocentric Chairmen. They issue instructions which nobody understands and nobody dares question. These autocrats automatically assume that because they themselves understand, others will. Everyone rushes around trying to carry out the instruction knowing full well they'll be reprimanded for making the wrong assumptions about what the Chairman wanted. C'est la vie!

The Superboss is very clear about what the company wants of him and very clear about how he's going to achieve it. What's more he makes sure his people are clear too. He chooses his words carefully, doesn't use loose terminology. He doesn't make ambiguous statements nor dither over a decision he finds difficult to make. He spells out what he wants and then checks with his people that they understand.

Conversely, when his people bring a problem to him, he makes sure he is totally clear about it. He doesn't make any assumptions until he achieves this clarity, questioning them thoroughly to make sure.

He makes it clear that expenditure has to be reduced by 5 per cent this quarter, that more time needs to be spent on the road with past, present and potential customers. He makes it clear he wants results.

ACTION TODAY

At 9.30 prompt this evening stop whatever you're doing, prepare your wife (husband, partner) a hot drink and invite her (him) to participate in a simulated workplace experiment. Switch on the tape-recorder.

You are allowed five minutes to explain the most important things you are doing at work at the moment. A further five minutes is allowed for questions of clarification.

Now turn off the tape-recorder, turn the television back on and enjoy your drink.

ACTION TOMORROW

At 9.30 prompt tomorrow evening ask your partner to stop whatever they're doing and make you a hot drink. Turn on the tape-recorder and ask your partner to repeat what you told her or him yesterday.

Compare the two tape-recordings. If there's total repetition then not only are you a Superclearboss, but you have a super partner. (Why should your partner be less clear about these important things at work than someone on the factory floor who works for you?)

REMEMBER

It is always clear what the SUPERBOSS wants and where he's going.

Climate

Every action a leader takes, every decision he or she makes, will have a direct impact on the climate in his or her organisation

Climate is how people feel about their boss and how they feel about the company. It can be hot, cold, stormy, sticky, warm or many other things. It can be a clear climate too.

Poor bosses give no time to their people, neglect them while pursuing more important matters such as financial planning, sales campaigns, engineering reviews or overseas trips. Their neglect creates a poor climate in their department, morale will be low, people will become demotivated. Their neglect will lead at times to a confusion about what they have to do, to a lack of resolution of daily problems. It will lead to a feeling that their contribution is not being recognised and to a dissipation of team spirit.

The Superboss aims to develop a warm, supportive co-operative climate where high standards are accepted and expected, where the team's objectives are crystal clear. The climate the Superboss seeks to create is one where every employee is totally committed to the company's goals and works hard to contribute towards them.

The Superboss therefore spends considerable time developing this climate, ensuring that people are clear about what is required of them, that their contribution is recognised and that the team is working well together.

He will frequently test the climate, sometimes directly by setting up a group and checking on a number of climate factors, sometimes informally by just strolling around and chatting to people. The Superboss can sense the climate in an office or on the factory floor by the way people are working, the way they behave towards each other, towards their boss as well as him. He can sense it by whether they smile or joke, or whether they look downright miserable. He can sense it from the degree of interest shown by the people in what he has to say, or by their moaning and groaning, or by their aggression.

ACTION TODAY

Check three key climate factors:

1 Is everybody clear about what they're doing?
2 Do they feel their contribution is recognised?
3 Do they work well together as a team?

Ask your Organisation Development expert, whether he be a consultant or a Human Resources specialist, to survey the climate. Do it informally at first, but if there is a problem commission a more formal survey. Give careful attention to the findings, and don't stick your head in the sand. Don't forget that you are the biggest influence on the climate in your area.

REMEMBER

For a SUPERBOSS climate is a key determinant of performance.

Commitment

Commitment doesn't guarantee success, but lack of it guarantees failure

There are a thousand managers who lack backbone – all experts in stating the problem but not in committing to finding a solution.

Commitment requires courage and taking risks. It means giving your all to other people, totally identifying with their goals.

Commitment cannot be imposed by the company. It is something that is self-generated, based on your own internal convictions.

Managers who lack backbone cover their options, duck and weave to avoid commitment. They'll talk forever rather than be pinned down. They're all too familiar. All words but no committed action. They would rather let you down tomorrow than commit to you today.

There are two components to commitment. The first is a commitment to another person. The second is to achieving a result for that person.

People respect a Superboss because he's prepared to commit to them as well as get things done for them. He's prepared to commit to his boss to producing an extra 4 per cent output next week, or commissioning that new plant within three months. He's prepared to commit to his people. He's prepared to commit that a new air-conditioning unit will be installed, or that a problem with travel allowances will be resolved. When the Superboss commits to a person to do something he will do it.

However, you will never find the Superboss committing to something he knows is impossible to achieve. He'll take a risk if there's an element of doubt, but if he's convinced it's impossible he won't commit. But that is rare. The Superboss demonstrates the art of the possible, achieving results which other managers may say are impossible. (How else could you land on the moon?)

ACTION TODAY

List your commitments to others – your colleagues, your boss, your people. If you don't have any commitments you and your company have a serious problem.

Check the list to ensure that you've honoured each commitment. If not, make sure it will be.

From now on, as a managerial discipline, whenever you're asked for a decision, or to pursue a line of action, make a commitment to the person who's asking. You must mean it, and you must follow through. If you don't trust yourself to remember, make a note of your commitment.

REMEMBER

Whatever the circumstance the SUPERBOSS always honours his commitments. The evidence is in his actions, not his words.

Common sense

The most intractable problems can be solved by common sense

Common sense is not obvious. It has to be challenged continually to avoid being turned into distorted sense.

Regrettably, too many managers lose sight of common sense, allowing themselves to furrow never ending ruts from which they can't escape. They collect the data, fill in the forms and follow the diktats from the centre without ever questioning what value this adds to the process of delivering excellent service and first-class results. Their language is peppered with management jargon which alienates them from their people. Nowadays they have to empower, re-engineer and think quality. They have to have missions, charters and other mindless bits of paper. They are forced to conduct 360° appraisals and pursue other highfalutin techniques imported from across the Atlantic. Those who dare to challenge these pseudo-scientific techniques are branded as cynics or mavericks. As a manager in a large organisation you are expected to lie down and be brain-washed by all this expensive nonsense.

The Superboss detests all these modern management techniques. He knows that under the brittle glossy surface of this fancy paperwork are some underlying common sense principles of management which go back to the year dot.

For the Superboss it is common sense to listen to his people, he doesn't need attitude surveys for that. It is common sense to give his people feedback on their performance, he doesn't need bureaucratic performance appraisal procedures for that. It is common sense to give high priority to communicating with his people, he doesn't need briefing groups for that. It is common sense to encourage his people to let him know what they think of his approach, he doesn't need 360° appraisal for that.

The Superboss is not against systems for improving productivity, measuring quality or measuring financial performance. What he is against is systems for managing relationships between him and his people.

ACTION TODAY

Audit all the modern management procedures you have to apply. Do they pass the common sense test? If not, abolish them.

Now write down what you think is common sense as far as everyday people management practice goes. Then ask one of your colleagues to challenge it. It should engender a lively and productive debate!

REMEMBER

The SUPERBOSS applies the 'common sense' test to every decision he makes.

Communication

Communication is not a panacea for all employee relations problems

It is naiveté of the highest order to assume that if you shovel more information down the organisation pipeline your employee relations problems will disappear. Yet I have seen such naiveté at the highest levels. It is the blind assumption that if you tell your employees what the company's problems are, if you tell them 'the facts', they will understand. Which is, of course, what they frequently fail to do.

In organisations rife with distrust, top-down communication campaigns will always be perceived by employees as company propaganda and brainwashing. Employees will be suspicious of the catch. 'They're trying to con us once more', they will say, or 'they're trying to soften us up again'.

To communicate effectively you must have trust. To achieve trust you must create an environment in which your employees can genuinely communicate with you, and you must genuinely listen and take the appropriate follow-through action.

Therefore the Superboss starts at the other end. He allows his people to communicate with him, allows them to ask questions on issues which interest them. He devotes time to it. If they're interested in the impact of exchange rate fluctuations on revenue then he'll tell them, but he won't force it down reluctant throats.

However, actions speak louder than words. You can have all the communications you like, but unless you take action nobody will believe the communication. The danger is the 'cry wolf' syndrome, or the 'mañana' mentality.

The Superboss never says anything he doesn't believe or doesn't mean. He would not say, for example: 'Unless we cut costs by 10 per cent the company will go out of business', unless he was convinced that it would. His communications carry conviction and that's why his people believe and trust him. Furthermore when they communicate to him they know he will genuinely listen, and will try to follow through with any appropriate action.

ACTION TODAY

Go down to the canteen at coffee break, or wander through the office when the tea's brewing. Chat to your people about communications within the company and how they might be improved. Listen carefully to what they have to say and follow up with any agreed action.

Be prepared for complaints like: 'We always find out through the grapevine'. (How are you going to be more effective than the grapevine?)

ACTION NEXT WEEK

Discipline yourself to plan all formal communications very carefully. If you're about to introduce an important organisation change, spend half a day thinking about the best way to communicate it, making sure the right people know at the right time.

Don't let the grapevine take over. It will distort things and reduce your credibility.

REMEMBER

The SUPERBOSS devotes over 80 per cent of his time to communications. When it comes to company communications, He *is* the company.

Competition

Managing people should be a balance between competition and compassion

Competition should be a spur to improvement. However, in any competition there are rules relating to morality, law, ethics and, if it's internal competition, company policy.

The Superboss encourages competition. He encourages his team to win each round and reach the top of the league. He promotes open competition, abhors behind-the-back 'political' competition. If he's managing the night shift, the Superboss will spur on his team to produce more than the afternoon or morning shift. He'll inspire them to achieve higher quality ratings. If he's the Regional Sales Manager, he'll inspire his team to beat the sales levels of all other regions.

The Superboss also encourages his team to compete against themselves, for example to beat last month's production record or revenue figures.

He encourages individual competition too, for example as 'employee of the month' in service environments. Even so he'll make sure that it's fair competition and that everyone has an equal opportunity to compete.

At a different level the Superboss wants his people to compete for promotion to other departments, for career development opportunities, and for the highest scores on training courses. He knows that for his company to survive in a harsh competitive world he needs to promote a competitive spirit among all his people.

However, in encouraging competition the Superboss will protect his team, will not allow anyone to ride roughshod over them, nor will he allow any individual to be sacrificed or destroyed in the process. Competition can only be healthy if it's combined with compassion and empathy for people. That's the balance between profit and people. One should never be at the expense of the other.

ACTION TODAY

Identify the competition you and your team are facing.

Create some competition to keep your people motivated. It might be a general knowledge quiz about the company. Or you can ask them to compete on attendance, time-keeping, quality, customer service compliments.

There are always a thousand opportunities to compete.

REMEMBER

For the SUPERBOSS competition is the spur to even greater successes.

Conflict

Conflict should always be on the surface, never beneath

The Superboss brings conflict to the surface, where it can be examined, studied and resolved.

The Superboss will sense the conflict. He might not see it at first, but he'll feel it bubbling, festering under the surface. He'll feel it by the way people talk, by certain snide comments, by frequent cutting remarks, by a stream of stroppy little memos.

Sometimes the conflict will be big, for example, over a pay differential between two sections. At other times it will be relatively small, such as some personal animosity between two members of the team.

As soon as he senses the conflict the Superboss will bring it to the surface. He'll try to elicit the facts and then the root cause of the problem. He'll bring together the protagonists around the table and open up with them. 'I could be wrong', he might say, 'but I sense we have some little problem brewing over the proposed transfer to Chapel House'.

When the conflict is exposed he'll keep the protagonists talking until everyone agrees on a solution. If that's not possible he'll ask them to agree that he should arbitrate and that his decision will be final. In dealing with conflict the Superboss never gets personal. He always keeps objective and never makes value judgements about the people holding the conflicting points of view.

Sometimes the Superboss has his own internal conflicts, for example when he believes the company is acting unwisely. He'll discuss them with his boss and try to keep an open mind. Unless he persuades his boss otherwise, he will ultimately have to accept the company's decision. If a conflict of conscience remains, he has only one option – that is to resign. And the Superboss will, and the company knows it. It never happens, because the Superboss thrives best where his principles accord with the company's.

ACTION TODAY

Think deeply about what's been going on in your department recently. Be completely honest with yourself (don't stick your head in the sand). Do you sense any areas of conflict or potential conflict? If so, call your team together and discuss your concern. Bring the issue to the surface and ask for their views, not only on the perceived conflict but how to revolve it. Then resolve it.

REMEMBER

When the SUPERBOSS is around there's little conflict.

Consent

To manage by consent is not to abdicate your responsibility, but to strengthen your authority

There is a myth among certain hard-nosed autocratic managers that to manage by consent is to be soft.

The fact is that management by consent is very hard and the only way any leader can get people to follow.

Consent concerns the exercise and acceptance of reason. The Superboss is reasonable and demonstrates it. Before he makes a decision, he'll attempt to gain a consensus by consulting his people. Having made a decision, he'll give reasons for it. Sometimes his decision will go against a certain group of people, but they will consent to it knowing that he has given them a proper hearing with careful consideration to their views, that he has exercised his authority in a fair and objective way, and that he had to make a decision which could go against them.

To gain consent the Superboss spends time with his people, explaining the complexities of the situation and the many contradictory factors influencing the final decision. He will seek their views and give weight to them. He will put himself in their shoes with respect to any issues affecting them. Similarly, he will ask them to put themselves in his shoes with respect to the decisions he has to make.

The Superboss knows that management by consent is not the same as management by permission. Never would he go to Personnel and ask permission for a change in staffing levels, nor would he go to his people and ask permission to install a new piece of machinery. He will seek their consent, but in the end he knows the decision will have to be his, for only he has the authority to make that decision, and only he carries accountability for it.

ACTION TODAY

Cast your mind back over some important decisions you've made recently which have had an impact on your people. Can you honestly say you sought their consent? Can you honestly say that they are behind you? If any decision went against your people's views, can you honestly say you went out of your way to explain why?

ACTION IN THE FUTURE

Discipline yourself to delay any decisions affecting your people until you've had an opportunity to gauge their views and seek their consent. But remember, seeking consent is not asking permission.

REMEMBER

Although the SUPERBOSS will always seek consent, he knows that it is rare for everyone to agree with his final decision.

Consideration

To give genuine consideration you must always put yourself in the other person's shoes

Many managers lack consideration for the people with whom they deal. They'll cut people short, not giving them a chance to open their mouths. They will pour scorn on others' ideas, making people look small. They'll neither listen nor pay attention when someone else is speaking. They'll turn up late for meetings, frequently messing you around.

Never the Superboss. He listens, he considers. He always puts himself in the other person's shoes and starts from there. He tries to understand how the person feels when talking to him.

He gives consideration to every individual he deals with because he respects that that person will have something important to say and furthermore will need to preserve an inner dignity, will need to maintain face in his eyes. The Superboss is so considerate he will never deliberately make another person look or feel small.

Giving consideration is not just a matter of showing humility, it's also a matter of finding and giving time to the person with the problem. The Superboss always finds the time for people. In a meeting, whether it be with one person or fifteen you won't see the Superboss dismissing a person's statement with his eyes; you won't see him frowning or showing signs of irritability when someone suggests a crazy idea.

The Superboss will consider all points of view. He'll encourage others to speak and then listen attentively, concentrating on what is being said, and giving it genuine consideration.

ACTION TODAY

Hold yourself back. Whoever comes into your office, let them do the talking. Say little, encourage them to talk and listen carefully. Put yourself in that person's shoes and consider their feelings and what they are saying.

Always assume that their motives are honest and that they are trying to say something important and furthermore trying to help the company. Never dismiss that contribution. Consider it and value it.

REMEMBER

The SUPERBOSS spends more time considering his people than considering himself.

Convictions

To have the courage of your management convictions you must be prepared to put your job on the line

This is the big test. This is when managers duck below the parapet and look the other way, or don't speak up when an injustice is being perpetrated by the company. This is when you disagree violently with your boss and vindictively try to sabotage his plans behind his or her back. This is when you stick your head in the sand and do nothing when that disruptive Billy Murphy starts stirring up trouble again.

This is when you prefer to patch a festering little problem, rather than take the more painful action to prevent the longer-term crisis. This is when you lack conviction.

The Superboss has the courage of his convictions. It gives him strength and the senior hierarchy knows it.

Convictions can never be imposed from above or by other people. They are deeply held beliefs that have evolved over a life-time of wise study.

The prime conviction of a Superboss is that his people should come first. They have a higher priority than anything else.

When an organisation attempts to force a Superboss to go against his convictions he'll take a stand and if necessary resign. But the Superboss tends to work for organisations which share his convictions.

ACTION TODAY

Go home tonight and discuss a hypothetical situation with your wife, husband or partner. At what stage would you be prepared to put your job on the line? Think carefully, you have a family and financial commitments. You know that other jobs aren't that easy to come by. Do you really have the courage of your own convictions?

Or are you one of those spineless creatures that float around large organisations like jellyfish, stinging other people but doing little else? Think of situations where you might have to put your job on the line. Would you? Would you? Would you?

REMEMBER

You can't become a SUPERBOSS without the courage of your convictions.

Co-operation

Is there any other way but to work together and co-operate?

The only alternative to working together is working against.

When someone is working against you it is not always obvious. Tasks take a little longer to be done, but you're not sure why. People forget to do things. More often than not lack of co-operation shows up through lethargy, through not being bothered, through lack of interest. Others will not put themselves out for you.

People don't co-operate because they're not with you. More than likely they're not with you because they don't think you're with them. 'Why should I bother with him? He doesn't bother with me except when he wants something.'

The Superboss seeks co-operation and gets it. He's with his people, not just in the task that has to be performed today, but in pursuing their interests, supporting them, putting himself out for them. The Superboss co-operates with his people in helping resolve their problems, and in return they co-operate with him. It's a two-way process, each side putting itself out for the other. You can't expect people to co-operate with you, if you don't co-operate with them.

The Superboss therefore always sets the example and takes the initiative in co-operating. He doesn't wait until he wants something and then ask for co-operation. If Tony Kidd wants his help in presenting a prize he'll co-operate. If Jessica Landor wants him to write a reference to the bank he'll co-operate. If his boss wants him to show round a visiting Japanese delegation he'll co-operate. In co-operating the Superboss will always show willing; he'll never throw up excuses and pretend it's all too difficult. He'll go out of his way to co-operate, to help the other person with whatever he or she wants.

ACTION TODAY

Make a list of the twenty people with whom you have to work most closely. Then rank them in order of co-operativeness. Forget the top ten, they're not a problem. Now look critically at the ten who are least co-operative and ask yourself why. If your answers are all to do with them, take another look at the lower list and ask yourself: 'Is their lack of co-operativeness perhaps because they don't think I co-operate with them?' Be ruthlessly self-critical; you might learn a lot and help yourself, and them.

REMEMBER

Many people co-operated to make him the SUPERBOSS he is.

Counselling

No manager can be his own counsellor

Contemplating your navel is fine and very necessary at times. However, your navel is not equipped to provide excellent counsel, which we all need on occasions.

Excellent counsel should always aim at helping the individual. For once profit and company should be forgotten.

When the Superboss sits down to counsel someone he only has one interest in mind – to help that person. He'll try to see the problem from his or her point of view. He might also hold up a mirror to the face, trying to reflect how the issue is seen in the eyes of others. By examining different perspectives the Superboss attempts to focus in on the problem.

Having held up the mirror he'll encourage the other person to talk further about the problem, even to suggest solutions. Only then will the Superboss offer his own advice, for what it is worth.

The Superboss also seeks counsel frequently. He will turn to his boss for guidance and advice. There will be one or two of his colleagues whose counsel he values greatly.

The Superboss also takes counsel from his subordinates, knowing that in many areas they have greater wisdom, insight and experience of the type of problem on which he needs help.

ACTION TODAY

Set up a series of person-to-person counselling meetings with individuals you know in your area (not just your direct subordinates). The purpose of the meeting is to focus on each person's specific interests (i.e. career interests, job interests, other work-related interests). Prepare carefully for each meeting. Think only of the person you're going to counsel and try to identify his or her specific needs and problem areas. At the counselling meeting be as relaxed, warm and informal as possible. Try to generate a constructive atmosphere. You are there to help that person. Anything he or she says to you should not be used in evidence against him or her.

REMEMBER

Always take counsel from a SUPERBOSS.

Creativity

It doesn't take much imagination to be creative

In the most exciting companies creative management is to the fore. Each supervisor, manager and senior executive will be creative, whatever the job or situation.

The process of giving birth to new ideas and pursuing them to implementation is one of the most exhilarating aspects of management.

Opportunities for creative management exist all the time. Any organisation that seeks to stifle creativity will eventually stifle its own further success, because outside its wall is a dynamic competitive world which is forever changing, forever threatening, forever challenging and forever requiring a creative response.

Creative managers thrive on these dynamics. The whole process of forming a superb team of people behind you requires the highest creative skills – to communicate effectively, to reward people fairly, to stimulate others to even higher standards of performance, and to fight the competition.

The Superboss is creative and encourages creativity. He is always seeking new ways of getting his team to work cohesively and effectively to meet daily challenges. He'll encourage his people to come up with new ideas and help find ways of pursuing them. It might be a new way of charting production output hour by hour; or a new hot-line company communication system; or a new service to the customer. It might be anything that helps the company achieve even more profit.

It might even be in the little things that happen every day at work. For example, there are a thousand creative ways of saying 'thank you'.

ACTION TODAY

Think of an idea for encouraging creativity among your people. Here's a suggestion: establish a two-monthly creativity session from a selection of staff at all levels in your area. Each session should last for two hours.

Divide the group (maximum 12 people) into two teams and put them into separate rooms. Each team should nominate a leader. For the first 45 minutes each team should brainstorm and then prioritise creative ideas to the other team.

For the next 45 minutes they should evaluate the feasibility of the other's creative ideas. The last 15 minutes should be spent briefly presenting the four evaluations.

You, as boss, then have to decide which of the four creative ideas you are going to pursue and implement (you can choose one, two, three or four of the ideas, but at least one). You must give your commitment to pursue the idea.

REMEMBER

For the SUPERBOSS it's creativity that helps create profit.

Credibility

It can take one minute and one decision for a manager to lose credibility – it will take years and a thousand decisions for that manager to regain it

Expediency is not compatible with credibility, yet many managers are expedient. They take the easy way out of a difficulty; an easy way out that is neither compatible with the long-term aims of the organisation, nor with what that manager has been saying these last few months.

Expediency results from a lack of backbone, a lack of clear thinking, a lack of an effective management philosophy, a lack of sincerity. Expediency leads to a loss of credibility in managers. They become 'all things to all people'. Their staff begin to run rings around them and the unions exploit the situation further. Their bosses and colleagues see them as a soft option and take advantage whenever they can.

To be an effective manager you must have credibility in the eyes of your boss, your colleagues and your people. The Superboss achieves credibility by being totally consistent, fair and firm. The Superboss achieves credibility because when he says something his people know he means it and he'll do what he says.

The Superboss achieves credibility because other people know exactly where they stand with him, because he is wholly predictable and reliable. You will never find a Superboss changing his arguments to suit his case, nor inventing reasons to justify a decision that has been made. The Superboss puts his money where his mouth is, so to speak. He is sincere.

The credibility of the Superboss gives his people a sense of security, of well-being. They know he will do his best for them. They know that he will only make painful decisions as a last resort and to that extent they will accept those decisions, trusting him. The manager who lacks credibility will find it nigh impossible to make painful decisions. Any attempt to do so will be fought every inch of the way, and more than likely he will back down.

ACTION TODAY

Don't eat anything at lunch-time. Let your stomach give you a little gnawing pain (it won't hurt you, millions are starving and experience far worse). Walk for half an hour taking the most scenic route, or drive to a park and walk for half an hour.

Take a deep breath and think very deeply and very honestly. Ask yourself the question: 'Do I have credibility in the eyes of the people around me?' You should be able to collect together in your mind a large number of clues and cues which indicate your degree of credibility. Compare, for example, the number of times people aggressively challenge your ideas and decisions as opposed to coming to you to seek advice. If you are not sure about your credibility rating you undoubtedly have a credibility problem. Start the long haul this afternoon.

REMEMBER

The SUPERBOSS achieves credibility by turning words into results.

Customer service

Never lose sight of why you are there – your customers will determine your fate

If excellent customer service were easy we would experience it every day of our lives. Yet it is so rare it tends to take our breath away when we do receive it.

Unfortunately customer service can never be relegated to a routine, to a mechanistic set of procedures, to a clever system or a programmed set of trained behaviours.

To maximise the probability that customers choose your products when your competitors' are just as good, your service has to be 'out of the ordinary'. In other words you have to achieve extraordinarily high levels of service day in and day out.

The Superboss has an ongoing obsession with customer service. He has total devotion to detail to minimise the possibility that some minor irritant might alienate hard to please customers. He makes sure that every single interaction with a customer whether by telephone, letter or face-to-face contact is as positive an experience as possible.

He ensures that every member of the team is 'on the ball' as far as customers are concerned, that each one of them goes out of their way to please every customer they come across.

He places exceptionally high value on customer service in every aspect of the management process, whether it be in recruitment and selection, in training, in performance management, in communications, in target setting or in your everyday behaviours.

He knows exactly what your customers think of you and the service you provide. The Superboss goes out of his way to solicit regular feedback from customers, whether they be external or internal.

The Superboss will drop everything to please a customer. He knows there is nothing more important. He sees his team as 'customer serving' (the inverted pyramid) as opposed to 'boss serving' (the traditional hierarachical pyramid).

ACTION TODAY

Be brave! Invite someone from another department to carry out a full audit of the customer service your department provides. Be prepared to learn the lessons!

REMEMBER

Never a day goes by without a SUPERBOSS thinking about his customers and doing something for them.

Decisiveness

To decide is to manage

The Superboss has an affinity for decisions. He loves making them and seizes every opportunity to do so.

He makes decisions virtually every minute of the working day – whether or not to visit Head Office on Friday, to go down at 10.30 for a quick coffee with Mike Appleyard, to raise last week's quality problem at the next team meeting, to send Joni Pollard on a special 3-day training course.

But every decision the Superboss makes has three aims. What is right for his people? What is right for his customers? And what is right for the company in terms of profit? If he's not clear he'll ask for more information, give the matter some further thought, consult a few people (his boss, employee representatives and others). Then, when he's clear about the impact on people and profit, he'll make a decision.

The real test for the Superboss, however, is whether or not he can make painful decisions, for example the occasional but necessary dismissal, or a lay-off.

The Superboss is prepared to suffer pain in deciding what's best for the company and its people.

There is one type of decision the Superboss never makes, a decision that could more effectively be made by his people. That's the art of delegation, which is covered in the next section.

ACTION TODAY

You're probably making more decisions per square foot of office space than you'd ever realised. So first of all just list the decisions you made yesterday, small or big. Study each one and question how it impacted profit and people. If you can't answer that, why on earth did you make a decision?

When you've finished studying this list prepare a second one. Include all the issues on which you did not make a decision yesterday. Study this second list and ask yourself what the consequences were of not making a decision. Can you honestly say there were no negative consequences, for example wasting more of your over-worked boss's time by asking him to make the decision for you, or alienating your people further with your indecisive procrastination? If your study does reveal some negative impact from your indecisiveness, reverse the situation immediately. Be positive, take a decision now.

REMEMBER

The SUPERBOSS always has a reason for his decisions. The reason is people, customers and profit.

Delegation

Delegation is the discovery that your people are 100 per cent more capable than you'd ever realised

You think you know it all. After all, you were promoted and they weren't. You know best. You want to make all the decisions. You're not confident your people understand; not confident they will do as good a job as you. Isn't it easier and faster to do it yourself, to make the decisions?

No! Because you're a Superboss.

The fact is, each member of your team spends most of his or her time on the job and is more expert at it than you think. The people doing the job tend to know best about it. If they think they can do better then they might seek your advice, but don't force it down their throats.

The Superboss lets his team do the job. He trusts them. He delegates all decisions about the job to them. He even gives them budgets to work with so that they don't have to trouble him with expenditure decisions in earning revenue.

Even so, he tends to be around most of the time in case they need him. He shows an interest but doesn't interfere. The Superboss knows that if he interferes he may as well do their job, in which case they can sit back, relax and put their feet on the table. (In badly-run companies this is called inefficiency.)

In delegating, the Superboss hands over the controls to his people. The last thing the Superboss wants to be is a 'control freak'.

ACTION TODAY

Question every decision you have to make today. Could it be made by one of your people? If so, refer it back and say: 'I think that's your decision, I trust you'll make the right one. If you need my help let me know.' Push as many of these decisions down as possible.

Furthermore, check today that every person in your team knows what he or she has to achieve in terms of business results. Then sit back and let them achieve it, encouraging them to make the appropriate decisions en route.

ACTION NEXT WEEK

Take the next two weeks off, delegating everything to your people, and discover how capable they are. Tell your boss you're attending a self-funded experiential self-training course on delegation at some hotel by the sea.

REMEMBER

The SUPERBOSS is as good as the decisions his people make, but no good at all if they don't make any.

Development

The keys to employee development are both personal interest by the employee's manager and self-interest by the employee

You can't impose development on an individual, he or she has to want it.

The Superboss knows that employee development is most effective when he takes a personal interest and gives it time. The Superboss will hold informal discussions with his people about their aspirations and development needs. He'll go to Personnel and take their advice about the best career move, say for Tess Weller or Stan Bishop.

The Superboss is prepared to lose his best people in developing them, encouraging them to transfer to other departments to gain vital experience and to apply for promotion out of his area. In addition to individual meetings the Superboss will sit down with his immediate team and rigorously review development opportunities for their more junior staff. They will always follow up with the agreed action.

The Superboss will encourage new recruits to develop by studying for professional qualifications, giving them time off for it, and even paying their fees.

The Superboss does all this and much more. He gets a great thrill out of seeing his people develop their careers and move on to take more senior positions. He has a reputation for providing an excellent training and development ground for the up and coming 'stars' in the organisation. To a certain extent people working for the Superboss will be seen as an 'élite', people who are going places. He sets high standards of performance and pushes his people to achieve them, thus creating opportunities to demonstrate their skills and giving them beneficial development experience.

The Superboss never holds his people down, is always encouraging them to develop. But he's honest enough to talk bluntly to those who have unrealistic career aspirations, who expect promotion within six months. He'll tell them to demonstrate some achievement over the next two years, then he might consider a career move for them.

ACTION TODAY

Plan a meeting with your team to systematically review everybody in the division, discussing their development and potential. Ask the Personnel Officer to attend, so that he or she can help you progress the actions agreed. You must follow through and implement these actions.

REMEMBER

You have to develop yourself continually to become a SUPERBOSS.

Discipline

The leader who has effective discipline in his or her team will never need to discipline anyone

Without discipline standards will erode. More people will arrive late for work, take extended lunch breaks, use company stationery for personal purposes, make private calls on the company telephone and 'expand' on expenses. And that's just at a personal level.

Company standards will also erode. Equipment will not be maintained, toilets not cleaned adequately, air-conditioning units not repaired. Customer service will deteriorate and profit will fall.

The Superboss believes in self-discipline. He applies it to himself and encourages his team to show it. From time to time he will review discipline in the department, looking at the degree to which standards are being maintained and the degree to which people accept and apply them. But he doesn't only review the discipline exercised by his people, he also reviews the company's own discipline in looking after its people.

The Superboss knows that discipline disappears when people feel the company is exploiting them ('The company takes us for granted'). That's when the people start exploiting the company: unofficial perks will proliferate, petty thieving will become endemic, corrupt practices will become the way of life.

The Superboss disciplines himself never to do anything which will be perceived by his people as exploiting them. Conversely he doesn't tolerate his people exploiting the company. He doesn't tolerate casual breaking of the rules, or lowering the standard of the enterprise. He quietly makes sure they all know the rules, explaining that they are there for a purpose, a good purpose.

The Superboss doesn't have people in his team who are deliberately going to break those rules. Everyone knows that the Superboss will severely discipline a person who transgresses. But in the Superboss's area this rarely happens.

ACTION TODAY

Put on the agenda for your next team meeting: 'Review of department discipline'. At that meeting quietly ensure that your people are clear about the discipline standards required and that they are accepted and applied.

REMEMBER

The SUPERBOSS believes in discipline, but is not a disciplinarian.

Dismissal

Dismissal is an admission of company failure

Dismissal is a grave issue. It can destroy people.

The Superboss will exercise extreme caution before any dismissal decision is made. He will check that all the proper warning procedures have been followed and that the person has had ample opportunity to improve. He will give him or her the chance to speak up and have his or her interests properly represented.

Above all the Superboss will be rigorous in ensuring that dismissal is fair and is handled in such a way that it preserves the person's dignity and minimises loss of face. He'll be thoroughly compassionate in his approach, knowing that back home families will weep and children retreat into a silence of insecurity and incomprehensibility.

Dismissal brings hardship and agony, and what is more it is often unnecessary, if not unfair.

As a process of social rejection dismissal frequently destroys the last vestiges of inner confidence, dignity and pride a person might have.

The Superboss will try his utmost to avoid dismissal. But he will dismiss. He will dismiss those who thieve, who are violent, who abuse the company (and thus its people). He will dismiss those who continually fail to perform despite a thousand opportunities to improve. He will dismiss when there is no job to be done. But always, he will search for a way out, a way to avoid the dismissal. It might mean demotion, or transfer to another department.

The Superboss knows that when the company hires people it makes a commitment to them. He will do his utmost to honour that commitment. Dismissal is a failure of that commitment, on both sides.

The Superboss will not tolerate hire-and-fire managers in his team, nor will he tolerate managers who do not confront potential dismissal situations.

Dismissal is a company failure, but regrettably failures sometimes occur.

ACTION TODAY

Make a mental note. Next time you are faced with a potential dismissal situation don't avoid the issue, but try to avoid the dismissal. Remind yourself that, whoever the person, he or she is a human being with a family and a face to maintain. So sit back, give the issue a little more time, think extremely carefully about it, consult your boss and your employee relations specialist. Then think again. But in the end you must decide. If the answer is dismissal, be scrupulous in handling it with dignity and compassion.

REMEMBER

For the SUPERBOSS, dismissal is a last and sorrowful resort.

Distance

To manage people successfully you have to walk a tightrope between being too close to them and too distant

Your best friend might live next door. You might go drinking at the same club together every Friday night. Your best friend might work in the same company as you.

How would you handle a situation where you were promoted to manage the department in which your best friend worked? What would you do if you discovered that his or her performance was so poor you had cause for dismissal?

You cannot stop people being friends at work, in fact it's desirable. As a result of promotion you cannot stop them being friends because one is now the boss.

There can be no hard and fast rules. For the Superboss it's a matter of judgement with respect to each individual case. He draws a clear distinction between relationships at the workplace and relationships outside it. It could well be that he has two separate relationships with the same person. At the workplace, he will be wholly objective and maintain the appropriate distance. He will not pass on confidential information to his best friend, nor abuse social confidences his best friend gives to him.

Even so the Superboss will try to avoid close social relationships with the people who work for him, at the same time trying hard to develop close and effective working relationships. That's the tightrope between proximity and distance. If the Superboss is president of the company football club he might drink beer with the team on Saturday night, but he'll separate that social relationship (albeit work-related) from the workplace relationships he has with certain members of the team. When it comes to management decisions he'll be totally objective and fair in dealing with a member of the football team.

ACTION TODAY

Consider your relationship with every person who works in your company, division, department or section. Can you honestly say that you treat each one equally, fairly and objectively? That you have not, in the last year or two, let a social relationship with an employee influence any decision you've made about that employee or others?

REMEMBER

The SUPERBOSS knows when to keep his distance and when to come closer.

Empathy

Without empathy for his people a manager will generate antipathy

A feeling is a fact. Everybody has feelings. Some show them, others suppress them.

One of the key skills in management is to identify, recognise and understand the other person's feelings. If they are negative (shame, guilt, inadequacy, loss of face, helplessness, rejection, embarrassment, self-doubt), help transform them into something more positive (pride, confidence, satisfaction, acceptance, joy, elation, goodwill).

The degree to which a manager can identify with and understand the other person's feelings is the degree of compassion he or she will have. The manager who neglects people's feelings does so at his or her peril. That manager will be shown to be a person who has no compassion, is ruthless and self-seeking and treats people like machines.

The Superboss feels for his people. He shows compassion when Hank Delale has to go into hospital for a varicose vein operation. He shows compassion when young Sandra MacLellan is shouted down by an aggressive team mate. He shows compassion when Meg Chaucer fails her accountancy exams. He shows compassion when his boss is made to look stupid in front of him. Such compassion is a reflection of the empathy he has for his people.

The Superboss exercises empathy by helping others understand their own feelings and eliminate the negative ones. He injects warmth, encouragement, support and help into the situation to alleviate the problem and give the person confidence. He will reassure Hank about the skill of the surgeons, reassure him that his job will be kept open for him. He will soothe Sandra and tell her that in his view she had a good point. He will tell Meg that you don't always win first time, and will encourage her to try again.

But there are always losers, and the Superboss has empathy with them too. He shows it when he occasionally has to dismiss a person, or when people lose a relative, or suffer permanent disability. He doesn't raise their hopes, in no way is he false. But the Superboss will do everything to help in these situations.

ACTION TODAY

Ask yourself, when dealing with any person today: 'How does that person feel?' You won't always know, but you might be able to find out. You might be able to demonstrate some compassion and be able to help. Always put yourself in the other person's shoes and try to develop empathy with them.

REMEMBER

It is with empathy that the SUPERBOSS energises his people.

Encouragement

Encouragement is a key source of motivation

Encouragement should be both genuine and frequent. You cannot just turn it on when you want something. That's a device, it's false and people won't believe you.

The Superboss is always encouraging his people, because he genuinely feels encouraged himself. 'At this rate of progress the order will be delivered two weeks ahead of schedule', he will tell them encouragingly. He'll call up a junior and say: 'I was really encouraged to learn about this great new idea of yours . . .'.

The Superboss will take the supervisor by the arm, walk him around, prop up the railing and look down at the assembly line. 'It's going well Bill', he'll say. 'The line is running smoothly, your people seem very keen, the housekeeping is excellent and what's more you've exceeded your targets each day this week. I'm encouraged Bill, after last week's fiasco you've turned it right around.'

To seek encouragement the Superboss is always looking for the positive things people are doing. He's desperate to encourage his people and puts himself out to do so for he knows that's the best way to motivate them.

And when things go badly he'll still encourage them, asking them to bear with him because he has faith that they will improve. And when the Superboss is around they normally do.

ACTION TODAY

Be encouraged and encourage. Go out of your way to find what is going well and then encourage the people involved. If you happen to come across something that is going less well, don't frown, don't criticize, don't moan, don't throw up your hands in despair – just give a little encouragement. You've seen it all before, you know it will improve.

Give some genuine encouragement, it costs nothing and is worth much.

REMEMBER

Encouragement is a key factor in the way the SUPERBOSS motivates people.

Enthusiasm

Enthusiasm is visible motivation

Lack of enthusiasm shows. It shows on people's faces and in performance, or lack of it.

The Superboss is always enthusiastic about his team and what they can achieve. His enthusiasm shows, becomes infectious.

The Superboss knows that enthusiasm is a positive force, a demonstration of the motivation to achieve.

The Superboss avoids false enthusiasm, knowing that it will undermine his credibility and he will be branded a 'con-merchant'.

His enthusiasm is always sincere and genuine. The Superboss is sincerely enthusiastic about the company (always stressing its good points, never playing on its weaknesses). He is genuinely enthusiastic about his people (knowing they can achieve so much). He is genuinely enthusiastic about the company's products and services (knowing they're the best).

He's enthusiastic about his work, showing everyone around that he enjoys it, that it gives him great satisfaction. He's enthusiastic about future challenges, about the prospect of overcoming problems.

His people love his enthusiasm, it makes them feel good, feel proud. It makes them enthusiastic in turn. The spirit of enthusiasm permeates the whole team.

But enthusiasm cannot be permanent. Occasionally the Superboss will feel low, dispirited. There will be a waning of his enthusiasm. His people will notice, will show concern. But they know how to lift him, make him enthusiastic again, for that's what he does with them when they're down and out.

ACTION TODAY

List everything to do with your work that you're enthusiastic about, examining in turn your company, your boss, your team, your colleagues, your company's products and services.

If you find you're enthusiastic about very little you have a serious problem. If you can't resolve it, then you must resign. You're no good to anyone if you're not enthusiastic about the company and your own contribution to it.

Now ask yourself whether your enthusiasm genuinely shows through. (You have to believe in something to be an enthusiast!) If you're not sure, it's because it doesn't show through, and this will be reflected in your team's lack of enthusiasm.

Starting today you must make sure you have some enthusiasm and also that it shows.

REMEMBER

The SUPERBOSS is a source of enthusiasm.

Example

A manager cannot avoid setting an example

If the example is to take two-and-a-half hours off for lunch and come back smelling of alcohol, then that's an example of how a manager values his or her time, an example of how he or she might expect others to behave.

If the example is to wear casual clothes in the office, then that's an example of the informal style the manager wants to establish.

If the example is to shout at people who are five minutes late, then that's an example of how the manager expects people to be treated.

Watch the Chief Executive. If he or she is polite, courteous, well-dressed, then that's an example of what is considered to be important in day-to-day behaviour at the office. Others will follow.

The Superboss sets a good example. He always behaves in the way he expects his people to. If he expects his supervisors to participate in safety training courses for operational staff, then he'll set an example and participate himself from time to time. If he expects each of his managers to produce a monthly one-page progress report, then he'll do the same and distribute it to them. If he expects his people to stay late on a Friday evening, he'll set an example and stay late too.

But it will always be a good example. You will rarely hear a Superboss using offensive language or running down the company. Furthermore the Superboss will expect his people to set an example. He'll expect his managers to volunteer for operational duty when others won't.

The most important example, of course, is results. The Superboss wants to set an example to the company of what really can be achieved when you have a superb team.

ACTION TODAY

Be personal. Ask yourself what example you set your team. Whatever you do, however you behave, whatever you wear, whatever you say, whatever you achieve, whatever you decide, that will be the example. Is that the example you want others to follow? Or do you think you should rest on your laurels and let them set a different example? Determine for yourself what example you really want to set, then be determined in setting it.

REMEMBER

A SUPERBOSS is a real life everyday example of good people management.

Expectations

Expectations, like mountains, should be high and visible

If others don't know what to expect, nor what is expected of them, they will not only be at a loss but feel extremely insecure.

The Superboss has high expectations of his people. He expects them to work hard, to be committed, to help each other. He expects them to be honest. He expects them to do their best all the time. He expects them to make mistakes, but to learn from those mistakes and do better next time. He expects them to let him know about problems they can't resolve, which might impede progress. He expects them to air their grievances with him rather than let them fester. He expects them to be creative and come up with ideas for improvements. He expects them to set exceptionally high standards and achieve outstanding results.

The Superboss expects a great deal from others.

And his people expect a great deal from him. They expect a Superboss to be fair and reasonable in all his dealings with them. They expect him to fight battles on their behalf, to consult them frequently, to communicate with them and let them know what's going on. They expect a Superboss to exercise his authority, to make clear-cut decisions. They expect him to take the lead in getting things done. They expect to see him from time to time. They expect him to make himself available and communicate with them. Most importantly they expect him to listen and understand.

When they talk to him they make their expectations clear, and he makes his clear to them.

ACTION TODAY

Set aside an hour in your diary (for today, tomorrow, or later, but it must be within the next two weeks) to spend with your immediate team to review expectations. Before you meet them prepare an 'expectation list'. There should be two columns:

1 What you expect of each of your team.
2 What you think they expect of you.

Keep the list short: each item should be no longer than one line.

When you meet the team ask them to list what they think you expect of them. Then ask them to list what they expect of you. If anyone asks: 'What do you mean by an expectation?' answer 'I expect you to make your own interpretation'.

Compare the various expectations. If there's a 90 per cent overlap you're probably a Superboss. If there's less, you've a lot to learn about them, and they about you.

REMEMBER

The SUPERBOSS expects no more than he is prepared to give.

Explanation

You cannot explain away bad management

Explanation is the safeguard against arbitrariness. However, if you've made a bad decision attempts to explain it away with invented reasons and excuses will severely undermine the credibility of management.

It happens frequently. A company will make a rushed decision at board level without thinking it through. The decision backfires on them. The board then seeks to find additional reasons to explain and justify their hasty decision.

An explanation that is invented after the decision is no explanation, but mere irrelevance. Nothing will reduce the credibility of management more.

The Superboss will only make a decision when he's confident of the reasons and therefore confident he can explain it to his people. It might be a zero pay increase, or a lay-off of a group of people, or a decision to change the shift roster.

However, there are certain decisions for which the Superboss will refuse to give detailed explanations. Whilst explaining that he selected the best person for the job, he will refuse to give more details as to why Wendy Morris was promoted and Jack O'Malley was not. He will refuse to explain why Peter Gorzel was dismissed yesterday. Confidential explanations will be reserved for the people immediately involved.

The discipline of providing sound explanations forces the Superboss to make consistently good decisions. It forces him to have the courage of his convictions. As a result he will be prepared to stand up in front of his people, or his boss, and account for his decisions.

ACTION TODAY

Set yourself a new discipline. Before you make any decision affecting your people, your boss, or your company, shut your eyes and imagine yourself explaining that decision to them.

If you are confident you can convince them, go ahead and make the decision.

If you are not confident you can explain, don't make the decision, and think again.

REMEMBER

The SUPERBOSS only makes a decision if he can produce a credible and genuine explanation.

Face to face

People problems are best resolved face to face

Managers who attempt to resolve people problems by remote control normally fail. It's little use pinning on the notice board an instruction from the Operations Director about overtime control. The Superboss will call his people together and explain, face to face.

If the weekly statistics show a decline in quality in Baytree Section the Superboss won't scribble 'What the hell's going on here?' on the report and send it back to Mike Appleyard, the quality control manager. Instead he'll call Mike to the office and ask him to explain face to face.

When Bob Keiller writes the Superboss a confidential memo saying he wants to discipline Liz Brodie, the Superboss will go to see Bob, face to face, and discuss the issue. He'll probably want to see Liz Brodie too, face to face, at some stage.

The Superboss knows that you cannot get to know people, nor they you, by writing memos or using the telephone. The Superboss therefore maximises the opportunity for face-to-face contact, whether there's a problem or not. He wants to understand about people. He wants to find out how genuine the are, what they're made of, what they're like.

The Superboss uses face-to-face contact for positive development reasons too. For example, if an excellent report comes his way from Paul West, a junior accountant, then he'll call Paul in for five minutes' face-to-face encouragement.

The Superboss encourages his people to face up to him too, that's why his door is always open, why he is never too busy to give time to people. The Superboss knows that effective employee relations are built on face-to-face contact and not by the remote application of hi-fi personnel policies and instructions from above.

The Superboss knows that face-to-face contact is a key to managing people successfully.

ACTION TODAY

Ask yourself how many new face-to-face contacts you have made during the last seven days. If the answer is zero, you're not a Superboss. Set yourself a target of making at least one new face-to-face contact with someone in your company each day.

REMEMBER

Everyone knows the face of a SUPERBOSS.

Facing the facts

The worst managers, which in my worst moments I think are the majority, suffer from the 'ostrich syndrome'

Stick your head in the sand, don't face the facts. Look the other way, duck, weave and avoid the problem.

But not the Superboss, he faces the facts.

When Burt McManus starts running down the Chief Executive in front of the Superboss and the team, the Superboss doesn't allow it to go unchallenged. After the meeting he'll take Burt aside and speak with him quietly and firmly to face the facts. 'What did you hope to achieve with your critical comments?' he asks. Burt might squirm and wriggle but he'll soon learn that moaning and groaning about senior executives achieves little but antagonism. If he has a problem with the Chief Executive then he should go and see him and face the facts with him.

When your Employee Relations specialist, your local staff representative and a few others keep advising you that communications are poor in your department don't go on the defensive. Don't tell them that you brief your team once a month, as if the Employee Relations person and staff representative were idiots not to realise you were an expert in communication. Listen, learn, explore the problem with them and face the facts. It might be you who is the problem. Then you'll learn. You'll have faced the facts. The way to become a Superboss.

There's that new secretary, Kate Honeywood. She's always ten minutes late, always chatting, takes hours to type a memo. You don't like to mention these things to her for fear of damaging the relationship. Be pleasant to her and face the facts. 'I could be wrong', you will tell her, 'but I just feel uneasy about your time-keeping, your chatting, the time it takes to type a memo'. She'll learn because you're a Superboss. A feeling is a fact. Face the facts. You could be wrong! You're a Superboss.

ACTION TODAY

This will be painful, so don't let anyone see. Hide yourself away and search those uncomfortable corridors of your mind for things that really worry you at work, that you don't like to face.

Then face them, even if it means being honest for the first time with your boss, or someone in your team.

But first jot down your worries and analyse them carefully. Make sure you know what you're talking about. Then face up to the people who give you these worries and discuss the issues with them. You'll be surprised at the outcome. You'll feel better afterwards and your performance will improve dramatically.

REMEMBER

A SUPERBOSS is never frightened of the facts.

Fairness

A manager can be right, a manager can be wrong, but a manager should never be unfair

Unfairness is a perception. It is a perception that you have recruited your old buddies from a previous company and unfairly discriminated against equally suitable people from within. It is a perception that the Chairman was able to afford a brand new Rolls-Royce at the same time as clamping down on pay increases because of a decline in the business. It is a perception that you sacked Nick Baker because you had a grudge against him after the Peters incident.

The perceptions can be, and often are, wrong. The Superboss goes to extreme limits to make sure that all his decisions are fair and furthermore are perceived to be so. He goes out of his way to see that personal prejudices (of which, like most human beings, he has many) never intrude upon his decision making, never show up in conversation.

Furthermore the Superboss will stand his ground to ensure that his people are fairly treated. If Adele King's application for a transfer to Customer Relations is handled in an unfair and negligent manner, the Superboss will fight like mad to get her a fair hearing. And if one of the company's South African staff has his home robbed and vandalised the Superboss will go out of his way to ensure he is fairly treated.

The way the Superboss treats John is the way he treats Mary, and the way he treats Mary is the way he treats Singh, and Pamela and Umara, and everyone. His principles never vary in the way he behaves towards people. If it's fair to give written warnings for poor performance in the UK, then it's fair to give written warnings in the USA, Germany, Ghana and Australia.

ACTION TODAY

This is an issue where perhaps you need the advice of the one closest to you. Go home this evening and discuss with your spouse (or partner or closest friend) whether or not they think you are perceived as a fair boss. Tell them about the various personnel incidents you've handled over recent weeks. Tell the truth about these incidents. Tell him or her about your doubts, your thoughts, your motives, the way you handled each incident.

As you spill the beans you might realise (and your partner might detect it) that on one or two occasions you've been less than fair. That will be a lesson.

REMEMBER

You'll have to be fair to a SUPERBOSS because he'll always be fair to you.

Fear

You cannot avoid fear as a motivating force, but you should not capitalise on it

Management by fear has a certain Orwellian sound. Nobody should manage by fear. Having said that, fear in organisations frequently exists.

Some fear the arbitrary and irrational decisions certain managers make. Some fear the widely fluctuating moods of their temperamental bosses. Others might fear that the actions of senior executives will drive the company out of business, that the extreme risks they take will put their jobs at risk. Liz Gerhard might fear that because she doesn't have the right sort of chemistry with her boss that he might think she's not capable of doing the job and peg back her salary and career progression as a result. She might even fear she'll be fired.

The Superboss is sensitive to the fears of his people. Wherever possible he'll try to reassure them. What he will never do is exploit these fears. He will never threaten his people or, to put it bluntly, put the fear of God into them.

If there's a fear a key customer might switch to a competitor, the Superboss will acknowledge that fear and try to reassure his people that the company is doing its best to retrieve the situation.

The Superboss is aware that fear is often based on ignorance, speculation, gossip and prejudice. He tries to overcome this by giving his people the facts as best and as soon as he can.

If a Superboss senses that his people have personal fears then he'll address them. For example if he senses that Alana Miles is fearful of speaking up at meetings he will try discreetly to help by encouraging her to be a little more assertive.

But certain fear will exist and should not be removed. The Superboss will tell his people: 'Have no fear, if you don't perform I will take action'. Employees should go in fear of breaking company rules, of abusing their colleagues, of not doing their best for the company.

The biggest fear however never relates to external forces but is the fear from within, the fear of oneself. That is the fear that the Superboss has conquered and helps others to conquer.

ACTION TODAY

Take your Employee Relations specialist for a walk after lunch. (Buy him or her lunch first.) Ask what he or she thinks your people fear most at work. Push and probe and try to identify as many fears as possible. Then talk to one or two of your team about these fears. Modify the list as appropriate and separate them into 'fears that can be addressed' and 'fears that cannot be avoided'.

Give priority to addressing the former. Your people will work more effectively for it.

REMEMBER

The only thing you should fear about a SUPERBOSS is his honesty and fairness in dealing with you.

Feedback

Performance feedback is essential to performance improvement – without it, performance deteriorates

I have yet to meet a single person who doesn't want to know how well he or she is doing. We all want reassurance that the contribution we're making is not only recognised but is the required one.

Without feedback people start making assumptions as to what is wanted of them, about standards, about how to behave. Without feedback team cohesion starts to dissolve and performance starts to deteriorate. Without feedback people begin to delude themselves that they're on course when they're way off track.

The Superboss gives feedback on a day-to-day basis, to his boss, his colleagues, his subordinates. Sometimes it's feedback on what he's been doing: this morning's negotiations, his visit to Binley's yesterday, his meeting with Adrian Sikes at lunch time.

At other times it's feedback about individual performance: 'I thought that was a good report, Rita, although it would be helpful to have a summary to begin with'. He'll take Ken Stevens by the elbow: 'I know you work hard, Ken, but let me give you some feedback. If you treat customers in the same abrupt aggressive way you treat your team mates then we have got a big problem looming up'.

He'll see Elena Morales and tell her: 'I thought you made an excellent presentation to the Chief Executive yesterday. He told me he was really impressed.'

The Superboss knows that without constant feedback he cannot reinforce what he values as important for the team. No feedback from a boss means that he is not bothered with you and is more concerned with other things.

ACTION TODAY

Walk around your patch and give some informal feedback to at least five people, whether or not they report directly to you. Try to be as positive as possible, looking for the good things they are doing. But don't avoid the negatives. Your people will appreciate your help if your feedback about 'negatives' is given in a positive constructive helpful manner.

REMEMBER

You cannot be a SUPERBOSS without soliciting genuine feedback from others and learning from it.

Fighting

Fight for your people, your customers, your company, your principles – but don't fight amongst yourselves

You only have to put your ear to the ground in most organisations to hear the fighting.

When a team starts fighting amongst itself the results can be disastrous, albeit excellent for the people you're supposed to be fighting – your competitors in the marketplace. Internal fighting dissipates energy, is inefficient, saps morale and is a reflection of extremely poor leadership. Such fighting often comes through indirectly as bitching about others, doing others down, automatically disagreeing whatever the merits of the case. Often the fight is with other departments or the centre of the organisation.

The Superboss will not allow members of his team to fight each other. He'll bring them together, if necessary bang their heads together, but in any event he'll get them working together as opposed to working against each other.

The Superboss will fight battles however. He'll fight to ensure that his people receive a fair pay rise this year, that they have adequate tooling and working conditions. He'll fight to obtain a sensible allocation of budget for training. In fighting for his people the Superboss won't give up at the first round. He'll fight to the bitter end if he believes he's right and it's for the rights of his people.

Often the battle will be one of principle. If his people are being discriminated against in the allocation of office space he'll fight on the principle of fairness and equity. If they are being unfairly discriminated against in the battle for promotion because of the bad reputation of his predecessor, then he'll fight against prejudicial selection.

Although the Superboss will fight on the issues of rights, he knows he is not always right. He knows when to accept authority and when to challenge it. The Superboss is far from being an extremist or a militant.

ACTION TODAY

List the battles you have fought and won over the last few months. Are there any? Are there many? What lessons can be learnt

Now look to the future. What causes are you going to fight for over the coming period?

REMEMBER

The SUPERBOSS never fights unless he's forced to fight, but when he does he fights to win and win he does.

Firmness

To be firm is to know when to stop listening and when to insist

The problem with many managers is that they stake out a position too early. They make promises they cannot fulfil. They issue threats which everyone knows cannot be carried out. When pressure is put on that position they cannot hold firm, they have to bend.

Other managers ignore problems, or accept explanations too readily. They accept excuses and do not attempt to find the root causes of problems. These are managers who do not hold firm on certain key principles of management They allow people to pull the wool over their eyes, or to cover up. They even turn a blind eye when standards drop, when people start abusing the company, stealing, taking longer rest periods, coming in late.

The Superboss has certain principles on which he will always hold firm and his people know it. Within this framework of principle he will give others plenty of scope to follow their own initiative.

The Superboss will never stake out a position too early and retract it later. He would not, for example, insist on reducing the staffing level on a machine only to find later it was wholly impracticable, as his staff had been telling him all along.

The Superboss only takes a decision if he knows he can hold firm on it. If he suspects that he might have to bend on a potential decision, he won't make it. He would not, for example, issue a disciplinary warning if he had any doubt that it might not hold firm on appeal.

Being firm means being sure. It means that you are confident and that others will be confident in you. If you don't hold firm, people won't know where they stand and will push you all over the place.

Occasionally the Superboss will make a mistake and not be able to hold firm on a decision. He'll then admit his mistake and change the decision.

ACTION TODAY

Make a critical review of some of the key decisions you've taken over recent months. Have you had to retract on any? If yes, ask yourself: Why didn't I hold firm? Did I admit my mistake? If there were additional factors arising after you made the decision, why didn't you take them into account before you made the decision? Discipline yourself never to make a decision unless you are completely confident it will hold firm.

REMEMBER

In being firm a SUPERBOSS is always fair and consistent.

Flair

Managing people successfully requires flair, a certain 'je ne sais quoi' or panache

Flair is the ability to deal with the unexpected. It is the opposite of mediocrity.

Dull managers are predictable, unimaginative. You know exactly what they're going to do – be unexciting, monotonous, mundane, boring and frequently negative.

The Superboss can be predictable too. He's predictably reliable, predictably firm, fair and consistent. You can predict that he's going to do his very best for the company and its people.

But within that framework of predictability the Superboss will demonstrate a high degree of flair for managing people successfully. The Superboss has a flair for winning you to his side. For example, he'll take you into his confidence when you least expect it. He'll give you support when you thought he had more important matters on his mind. He'll come and seek your advice when you expected him to go elsewhere. The Superboss has a flair for making your work exciting, interesting, a flair for making you feel good about what you do, a flair for making you feel important.

The Superboss also has a flair for reaching the heart of a problem. Whether it's his instinct or his greater experience, he always seems to arrive at the unexpected solution when everyone else has given up. He has a flair for overcoming obstacles and seeing his way through to the end. His team might be despairing as to how they can achieve further cost reductions, but the Superboss has the flair for finding that little pot of gold (unused stock) which has been overlooked.

And how does the Superboss develop flair? There's no single answer. He has a nose for a problem, an eye for a detail, an ear for the other person. He has tasted success and has a touch of class. By developing his senses he has developed an instinct for winning people to his side, for overcoming problems, and for reaching the finishing post first. His flair will probably derive from a distillation of his experience, knowledge, skills and his enthusiasm and awareness of what's going on. It will also come from the exceptional efforts he takes in pursuing high standards of professionalism.

ACTION TODAY

Think of one person in your company, whether or not he or she reports to you, who in your opinion demonstrates flair. Carefully observe and study that person from a distance. Try to analyse why that person has flair. Try to learn from his or her approach to work.

REMEMBER

The SUPERBOSS has a flair for working with people, a flair for cracking problems and a flair for achieving great results.

Focus

Keep in focus whatever you have to deliver

We live in a highly stressful world with an unrelenting stream of pressures cascading down on us every day to distract us from our main goals. We are forever being summoned to urgent meetings, our phones ring incessantly, there is always a queue of people waiting to see us and then there is that ever increasing pile of paper in our in-trays.

The danger is that we become wholly reactive and allow ourselves to be driven by events. With such reactivity we can easily lose control. Suddenly things begin going wrong, matters worsen and we are in a vicious downward spiral. We can see it in many organisations. They become crisis driven, dealing only with emergency after emergency.

The Superboss avoids this potential mayhem by keeping focused on what he has to achieve. He is clear about his goals and never loses sight of them.

He knows he has to deliver and is absolutely determined he will. By hook or by crook he finds a way to achieve the results to which he is committed. In doing so he does not allow himself to be distracted by unnecessary meetings, irrelevant bureaucracy or meaningless demands from the centre. He focuses on motivating his people to deliver the finest service possible to their customers and thus achieve the bottom-line results required of him.

When the Superboss promises to bring in an important project on time and within budget he does so. He just focuses all his energies on the vital activities necessary to deliver this result.

In other words the Superboss always has in mind what he has to achieve, and never lets it slip out of mind.

ACTION TODAY

Bring into focus what you are here to achieve. Write it down. Test it on your boss. If he or she agrees it's in focus! Test it on your people. If they disagree or don't understand it's out of focus!

As you progress you will need constantly to reset your focus to ensure the end destination is still in view.

REMEMBER

The SUPERBOSS keeps focused on the end result.

Follow through

Follow through and your people will follow too

It happens when you follow through. It happens to be what you said you'd do.

Many don't. Bob Lewis said he'd send you a copy of the Stage 3 report and didn't. Barbara O'Donnell said she'd phone back to confirm that booking, and didn't. Gary Cordello said he'd drop by with the proofs and didn't.

They didn't follow through, but the Superboss will. He'll allow them a little latitude, then he'll phone Bob, Barbara and Gary.

When Steve McPherson says Training Department still haven't introduced the Health and Safety course they promised him six months ago, despite frequent reminders, the Superboss follows through on behalf of Steve.

The Superboss knows that if he doesn't follow through, nobody will. He sets the example and his people follow, because if they don't he'll be following through and asking why.

But it's more than that. When Frank Michner mentions that he's going into hospital next week, the Superboss follows through, finds out how he is, sends some magazines and a card, stops by to see him when he returns.

When Chan Uttal says that Personnel seem to be procrastinating over the recruitment of a new clerk, the Superboss follows through. He'll ring Chan in two days' time and ask how she is progressing with the recruitment, and if she's still having problems he'll follow through with a phone call to Personnel on her behalf.

And when the Superboss promises Hassan Sameer some training in finance for non-financial people he'll follow through and make sure he receives it.

ACTION TODAY

Call in your secretary and make a systematic check through your diary for the last few weeks. Try to recall what happened at each meeting you attended. Try to remember if you promised to follow through on anything, and whether you actually did. Check your recent mail the same way. Follow through immediately if you've forgotten to do so.

ACTION TOMORROW

Cast your mind back over recent informal encounters with your people. Is there anything they mentioned to you which perhaps you should now follow through?

ACTION NEXT WEEK

Create a reliable follow-through system to ensure that you honour all the promises you make and check up on all the actions you say you're going to take (as well as on other people's promises to you).

REMEMBER

You can rely on the SUPERBOSS to follow through.

Fun

The precursor to fun is hard work

Some people live for fun, and it's not funny, because they destroy their lives. The pursuit of fun degenerates into an orgy of self-indulgence.

For the Superboss fun is never an end in itself but a consequence of all the hard work he and his people do. It might be fun to run in the London marathon but it is painful and arduous. It might be fun to play your part in a local theatrical production but it requires hours of preparation and rehearsal to meet the high expectations of the audience. It might be fun to work for a Superboss but it also involves strenuous effort to deliver to the highest levels of performance to meet customer requirements.

Fun is a by-product of all the hard work people put into their achievements. It's an expression of delight and joy when a problem has been overcome, when a main objective has been met.

Fun can also be a mechanism for bonding people together and spurring them on to overcome obstacles and reach the winning post. But fun should never become the permanent focus because then it diverts from the delivery of the real goals and becomes an end in itself.

The Superboss encourages fun at work. He encourages competition, socialisation and creative trivia. He'll run a product knowledge competition amongst his staff and give a bottle of something to the winner. He'll take the team to TGI Friday's for dinner when they've had a good month and he'll joke with the best over a bottle of beer. And he'll create trivial ways of reinforcing positive points, a cartoon here, a crazy badge there and a smile everywhere.

The Superboss wants people to enjoy themselves, to take a delight in coming to work, to get a buzz from pursuing an exciting goal. But the focus must be the end result that has to be achieved. The enjoyment, the delight, the buzz and fun are necessary by-products of all the hard work. High quality, excellent standards of service and stunning profitability are the product of a disciplined approach to work. Discipline is not incompatible with fun but can be at the mercy of it.

Inevitably there has to be a balance, and it is the Superboss who finds that balance. All play and no work is as bad as all work and no play.

ACTION TODAY

Find out from your people what makes for fun in the work they do. Then enhance that fun but without taking your eye off the ball.

Try to create fun as a consequence of hard work, discipline and achieving spectacular goals. Fun can be hard work made exciting and it can be a spectacular celebration for achieving a spectacular goal. What it cannot be is an end in itself.

REMEMBER

The SUPERBOSS never makes fun of people, but makes it fun for people to work hard for him.

Gestures

Every gesture you make is a signal to your people

Gestures can have a very positive impact. A gesture can be sending a card to someone who is sick, or a thank-you note to someone who has rendered particularly good service to the company.

A gesture is a wink to someone who knows, a light slap on the back as a measure of appreciation (but take care to avoid any hint of sexual harassment). A gesture is an extra day off for someone who voluntarily worked late without overtime pay.

The Superboss makes genuine gestures. They are unexpected but positive behaviours, never predictable and never taken as a right. They tend to be small but magnanimous movements in another person's direction. Gestures are made without request, without negotiation and without trial. Gestures are a token of trust, a demonstration that the Superboss is prepared to 'give a little' without asking.

Gestures give the Superboss power. They cost little in time or resource but are of immense value in motivating people. But they have to be positive and they have to be genuine.

As a gesture of appreciation the Superboss will take his team for a Chinese meal on meeting an important deadline. As a gesture of welcome he'll pen a personal note at the foot of the transfer offer to Anjana Patel. As a congratulatory gesture he'll send Lucy Kendal a bottle of champagne when she passes her accountancy examinations second time round. As a gesture of concern he'll phone Mohammed Ibram at home when he's laid up on his back, and ask if there's anything he wants done.

Ultimately every behaviour is a gesture. The key for the Superboss is to be aware of the gestures he makes and to ensure that they are positive.

ACTION TODAY

Make a gesture today. A positive gesture. Bring in some chocolate for the team on reception – most people take them for granted, but not you. Send hand-written thank-you notes to the engineer who worked to midnight to get the new multitracking system working again and to the young graduate who worked so hard over the weekend to reduce the amendments backlog. Find a minute to go and see the people in customer services who've had a really rough time recently.

REMEMBER

The SUPERBOSS goes out of his way to make positive gestures towards his people.

Giving time

A manager's highest priority is to give time to his or her people

The worst managers are those you cannot get in to see, whose secretaries are haughty obstructionists (to say the least).

The worst managers are those who give little time to their staff; who are always in meetings with the president, or visiting Saudi Arabia, San Francisco or Singapore, or writing speeches, or dealing with some urgent problem down at C Plant. They are the managers who would rather be studying reports on new product evaluations than seeing people; who would rather be having expensive three-hour lunches with customers than appraising people. They are the managers who come in at 9 am and shut themselves away in their offices, behind closed doors, only to emerge at 5.30 pm.

The Superboss has an absolute rule. Unless he is on vacation or away from base and uncontactable, he will give time to any of his people within 24 hours of their asking for it. No matter how busy he is, no matter how crammed his diary, if Mona Aziz wants five minutes of his time, he will, without question, find her five minutes of his time within 24 hours. It might have to be at 8 am, or 6 pm, but he'll go out of his way to give her the time.

But the Superboss doesn't wait to be asked. He finds time for circulating so that people can raise any issue they like as he passes by.

For the Superboss giving time to his people is the most important thing he can do. It is his people who deliver the results, who have the problems, who need his help. He'll therefore give time to all aspects of managing people, to their selection, to their training and development, to their motivation, to solving their problems, to communications and to their welfare,

He'll give time as well, of course, to his boss and his colleagues. He finds the time by not over-committing his diary, by not attending unnecessary time-consuming committee meetings and, I'm afraid, by not working strict 9 to 5 hours.

ACTION TODAY

Look back over your diary for the last four weeks. How much time have you genuinely given to your people? At least 80 per cent should be on people issues, and at least 40 per cent should be made freely available to them one way or another to raise any issues and problems. Should you be nowhere near 80 per cent 'people time' and 40 per cent 'availability time', then more than likely you will have serious people problems in your area.

Always create blank slots in your diary when you can devote time to your people.

REMEMBER

A SUPERBOSS reflects the way he values his people in the time he gives them.

Glory

The glories of management are never visible

Anyone who owns up to being a Superboss is not a Superboss. He or she is a glory-seeking surface manager. No Superboss will ever admit to being one.

A Superboss doesn't seek glory. He has sufficient faith that his time will come for promotion, for salary increases and that in due course those who make such decisions will recognise his super contribution. If such decisions don't come his way, if he's passed over for promotion, or doesn't receive the salary increase he thinks he deserves, then he'll try to understand why, try to learn a little, try to do better next time. And if he concludes it's a bad decision, he'll put it down to Fate. Everybody makes bad decisions from time to time.

The Superboss is more interested in the glory of his team, identifying their successes and giving them credit. He never takes credit himself. He goes out of his way to recognise outstanding performance by members of his team and is wholly objective in doing so. The Superboss always avoids the 'blue-eyed boy' syndrome.

When the Chief Executive comes to address the department and congratulate them on their fine performance last month, the Superboss in reply says it was all due to his team.

The Superboss knows that glory is something that is given, not taken. He is not impressed by those who keep telling him they are doing a fantastic job. He'll take them aside: 'Don't you trust me? Why do you keep telling me you're doing a great job? Isn't it my job to know? When you're doing a great job, I'll tell you.' And the Superboss will.

ACTION TODAY

Make your team feel proud, give them some glory. If you can't, what are you doing? Aren't they any good? Feature them in the company newspaper, or draft a letter for the Chief Executive to sign thanking them for having pulled out all the stops to complete that export order. Or when Jane Smith comes in on Monday to tell you she's completed the London marathon in record time (for her), call the team together, congratulate her. Give Jane Smith some glory, she deserves it.

REMEMBER

The SUPERBOSS knows that those who seek glory never achieve it.

Grievances

Not to have a grievance procedure is a failure on the part of management – to use it is also a failure on the part of management

The grievance procedure must be there as a safety valve. But it should be used rarely.

The Superboss creates an atmosphere in his department where people feel free to air grievances. He doesn't make them feel threatened, or guilty, or silly if they raise a grievance. Thus if Reuben Zabaleta has a grievance against a colleague the Superboss will hear him out, even if the grievance appears to have little justification.

If someone raises a grievance with him, the Superboss will give it his highest priority. He'll create time within 48 hours to look at the problem and try to resolve it. He'll draw in other people and then he'll refer back to the person with the grievance as soon as possible.

If the grievance is outside his own jurisdiction, for example, about lack of car-parking spaces for disabled people, or about the office always being locked on a Saturday when an employee wants to work voluntarily, then the Superboss will pursue the grievance on behalf of the employee, taking it up with the appropriate person. The last thing the Superboss will say is, 'I can't sort out car parking, that's not my responsibility'. Nor will he say, 'If you're crazy enough to want to work on Saturday you will have to work at home'.

The use of the formal grievance procedure in an organisation is, in the Superboss's eyes, the failure of the supervisor or manager to whom the grievance was first addressed. The immediate manager should be accountable for progressing and resolving any grievance before it reaches formal procedure.

ACTION TODAY

Have an informal drink with your immediate managers at lunch time or after work. Ask if they can recall the last time a grievance was raised in their area. Mention that you'd like to be aware of any grievances their people have. The last thing you want to happen is to walk around and be caught out with a grievance the manager hasn't reported to you.

ACTION TOMORROW

Go to Personnel and ask to see the company's grievance procedure. Examine it and make sure you understand it.

REMEMBER

Resolving grievances is a SUPERBOSS's top priority. How else can he ensure that his people are motivated?

Health

To put your business first, you must put your health first

Despite the continuing propaganda in newspapers, magazines and a vast selection of books, people continue to put their health at risk: at work, at home and elsewhere.

People who destroy their health inflict damage way beyond the confines of their body. They create immense problems not only for their families but also for the people they work with and society at large.

The Superboss recognises that certains aspects of health are beyond a person's control. We can do little about the air we breathe and nothing about the genetic makeup we inherit. However, there are many aspects of personal health over which people have total control. We make daily choices with respect to diet, drink, drugs (official and unofficial), exercise, life-style, leisure, education and how we conduct ourselves. All have an impact on our health.

The Superboss starts with himself as an example. He finds time to exercise, he moderates his diet, he avoids drugs (even those doctors dispense) and maintains a life-style which puts him in peak condition to discharge his many varied responsibilities.

He knows that if he is always taking days off for 'flu' there is a risk that others might try to emulate him. He knows that there are certain people who are never ill, who have not taken a day off work in twenty years whilst there are others who seem to be ill every other Monday.

The last thing the Superboss will do is attempt to impose his own personal healthy habits on others. All he wants is to set a fine example and be in the best condition to make the best decisions. There is always a risk that managers who are not feeling well will be less rigorous in evaluating all the options before making an important decision. Tiredness and ill-health can be incredibly dangerous for an organisation.

Where possible the Superboss will create opportunities for people to sustain their health, perhaps encouraging the canteen manager to introduce a healthy diet, or fixing a discount arrangement with a local leisure centre for use by his people, or persuading the company to pay for a regular health-check.

ACTION TODAY

Seek out a colleague who appreciates and understands the importance of health and ask this person to undertake a complete health-check for you. Urge him to be ruthless in his questioning relating to exercise, diet, drink, drugs, and life-style.

Tell the truth and don't become defensive. Never make excuses if he exposes some unpalatable facts.

You probably know the answers already. Face up to them.

ACTION TOMORROW

Becoming unhealthy is dead easy.

Keeping healthy is incredibly difficult.

Set yourself some health goals and aim for them!

REMEMBER

A SUPERBOSS is always fit to make decisions.

Honesty

There is a myth that managers who are too honest are politically inept and managerially naive

Nobody ever disputes it is dishonest to fiddle your expenses, put your hand in the till or tell lies on your career résumé.

But dishonesty in management is more widespread on the subject of the declaration of motives and the statement of opinions. It is often prevalent through the omission of certain facts and a gloss on the balance.

To mislead by omission is to be dishonest. Dishonesty in management is far-reaching because companies assume that business confidence will be lost if the naked truth (more losses, more disputes, more complaints) is told. This creates a climate of dishonesty and distrust throughout the organisation and beyond. One dishonest statement will lead to a thousand dishonest statements. No one will trust anything the company says.

Dishonesty among managers is present in companies stricken with politics. For example, the scheming manager who paints a very bleak picture of what is going on in another department when talking to the Chief Executive is being dishonest in failing to declare his motives: an interest in managing that other department. The manager who tells the boss that everything is going well, when the problems are numerous, is similarly dishonest. There are countless other examples: the manager who tells his staff he is looking into the catering problem when in fact he's forgotten all about it; the Financial Director who shuffles millions into 'exchange provision' to avoid the books looking too good before the pay round.

No person can be a Superboss by being dishonest in any shape or form, whether it be by misleading statements or blatant omission of the facts.

ACTION TODAY

Don't turn away from this page. Confess all now! To yourself. Whether it's politically inexpedient or not, ruthlessly purge yourself of every dishonesty, every distortion, every misleading statement and omission you've made over recent months.

Then make a vow always to be honest. Honesty pays, even if you have to lose your job in the process. A clean conscience and no job pays greater dividends than distortion and dishonesty at work.

REMEMBER

The SUPERBOSS is honest not only with those around him, but with himself.

Humility

Humility for a manager is a positive strength

The manager who knows it all has no humility. The manager who gives little time to others has no humility.

The manager who doesn't listen has no humility. The manager who never admits a mistake has no humility. The manager who is not interested in people's problems has no humility.

There are many such managers. They are merciless in the pursuit of their own selfish ambitions. They will push others aside, ignore them, neglect them, even destroy them in their merciless mission to get to the top.

They don't realise that their people want to go places too.

The Superboss will have the humility to respect this. He will have the humility to learn from them because he has the humility to acknowledge he doesn't have all the answers. He has the humility to accept that Ray Cotton can do a far better job supervising engineers than he ever could. Why should the Superboss even attempt to tell Ray Cotton how to do his job? That would be a total lack of humility.

The Superboss gains strength, credibility and respect because he has sufficient humility to learn from the Ray Cottons of this world, to accept their advice and help. In return the Superboss will go out of his way to help Ray Cotton.

Humility is the process of recognising your own several weaknesses and respecting other people's substantial strengths.

ACTION TODAY

When you sit in the bath tonight, think about your own weaknesses in relation to your management task, and then the strengths of those in your team.

ACTION TOMORROW

Take one personal weakness, show some humility and ask the person in your team who has the corresponding strength to give you some advice and help you.

REMEMBER

The SUPERBOSS has sufficient humility to know that he has as many weaknesses as his people have strengths.

Incentives

Individual incentives are incompatible with team spirit

The carrot and stick theory went out of fashion a long time ago. We'll dwell on carrots here.

If the company offered you an extra one week's salary for doubling your output tomorrow how would you react? Unless you're incredibly lazy (and why reward lazy people?) you would rightly reply that you're already working at maximum output.

Assuming that your current level of pay fairly reflects your current contribution, it is spurious to think that this contribution can be increased by paying you more. This would imply that you are not contributing as much as you should. If this is the case it is an issue of performance management, not pay.

Throwing money at performance problems is no substitute for good management practice.

The fact that sales people receive incentive payments and others in the same organisation do not creates enormous problems and inequities. What is the incentive for the person who masterminds the advertising, who organises sales support, who provides back-up customer services, who distributes the product, who designs the packaging?

These days, unless you're self-employed, you cannot work as a one-man band. Even sales people out on the road need a back-up team.

If there's to be any incentive the Superboss believes it should be a team incentive. With the exception of a company profit share incentive (available to all employees) the Superboss would prefer any team incentive to be non-financial. Occasionally he might say: 'Look, guys, there's an urgent job on this week, an extra twenty tons for Dennett's. If we can finish it on time by Friday close of play, there's a bottle of whisky in it for each of you.' Or he might say to his sales team: 'If we can win that contract with Billson's, we'll have a night out on the town'.

The Superboss knows that the application of individual incentives can be divisive, demotivating and counter-productive.

ACTION TODAY

Do a little gentle thinking. Think about yourself. Is there any incentive the company could offer you which would motivate you to improve your performance? If the answer is 'yes', consult your boss about your performance improvements – the answer probably lies in his or her hands.

Now think about your people. Is there any incentive you could offer them which would motivate them to improve their performance?

Is the answer any different from your first answer? If you say 'yes', you have a problem. You cannot allow incentives to be a substitute for your own management incapability

REMEMBER

The SUPERBOSS has such a high degree of self-motivation that he require little if no incentive to motivate him more.

Influence

Influence is only effective when it is a two-way process

In this highly competitive world there is a regrettable tendency towards 'macho' management in many quarters. It becomes a matter of pride not to be influenced by others, the preferred pursuit being to influence others, to 'win their hearts and minds', to 'sell ideas' (such as thinking quality) to the troops.

The process by which senior executives try to influence the people in their organisation soon becomes one of exhortation, brainwashing and propaganda.

There is good influence and bad influence. A Superboss influences his people by his behaviour, actions and decisions, but NOT by his words. Conversely, it is the words of his people which influence him.

It is fashionable in many organisations to solicit the views of people, to conduct attitude surveys, to find out what people think. This is great but only if the senior executives obtaining this information allow it to influence them. Too often the information is obtained and then discarded. There is no change and no improvement.

The Superboss is prepared to be influenced by his people. He is prepared to change his mind if they suggest a better method of rewarding people, if they suggest improvements in the approach to training, if they suggest ways to communicate more effectively.

When the receptionist Mary Green knocks on his door to express her concerns about security the Superboss does not dismiss them out of hand. He is prepared to listen and be influenced by her idea to have a panic button below the reception desk.

ACTION TODAY

When were you last influenced by your people? Make a note of all the times you have been influenced by them over the last four weeks.

If the answer is 'none' you can be assured that your reputation with your people is far from being a Superboss.

ACTION TOMORROW

Be brave. Call your people together and ask them this question: 'On what sort of things would you like to influence me?'

You may be surprised at the answer!

REMEMBER

A SUPERBOSS is always under the influence of his people.

Initiative

Taking the initiative is the first step to success

In a complex competitive world the opportunities for success are everywhere, but are often difficult to see. It takes initiative to spot them, seize them and exploit them.

The Superboss is full of initiative. He sees opportunities everywhere – for his people, for his company, for profit, for improvement. He takes the initiative and seizes them. For example, an employee might mention in passing that he has an idea for improving the stock control procedure. The Superboss will take the initiative and pursue the idea on the employee's behalf. For example, his people might be experiencing persistent problems with quality control. The Superboss will take the initiative, have a look, call in an outside expert and try to solve the problem.

The Superboss might see the opportunity for developing a new market in the North. He'll take the initiative to step into an aeroplane and size up the opportunity himself, developing his contacts in the process.

The Superboss also encourages initiative among his employees. He'll encourage initiatives to improve performance, to improve relationships, to resolve problems and to come up with new ideas. Should his people want to experiment with new maintenance schedules, he'll let them take the initiative. If they want to take the employee representatives away for a weekend seminar on employee relations, he'll let them take the initiative.

The Superboss will never stand in the way of initiatives.

ACTION TODAY

Take one initiative today (i.e. something you hadn't thought of yesterday) to manage your people more successfully.

ACTION NEXT WEEK

Identify what initiatives each member of your team has taken over the last three months.

ACTION NEXT MONTH

Review 'initiative' with your team.

REMEMBER

It takes initiative to become a SUPERBOSS.

Inspiration

It takes inspiration to climb out of the rut and beat the competition

There are greater experts on lateral thinking than me. But I've seen the disastrous results vertical thinking achieves. The well-ploughed furrows of attempting to crack a constantly recurring problem, the repetitive exhortations to improve efficiency, cut down costs and work harder.

I've seen the despair when the competition steals a lead in the marketplace with a new product; the despair when the unions once again respond threateningly and aggressively to the familiar pleas for pay restraint.

We all tend to become trapped in these rigid mind-sets, entrenched in a view that there is only one solution to a problem when all the evidence suggests that the solution is not working. Performance related pay is a classic example.

Companies, managers and people become trapped in ruts from which they seem unable to extricate themselves. But you don't have to look far for the inspiration to climb out of these ruts. There are always people in the organisation who will find the lateral solution.

The Superboss seeks inspiration through his people. He won't hack away at well-tried but demonstrably unsuccessful solutions. He'll be stimulating and inspiring his people to be creative, to think laterally, to produce new ideas, new approaches. He'll give them plenty of scope. He'll create a climate in which people can achieve inspired results.

For the Superboss inspiration is second nature. He's always searching for it and frequently finds it.

ACTION TODAY

What inspires you?
Who inspires you?
When are you inspired?
Why are you inspired?

If you're never inspired, have an inspired guess at the answers to these questions.

Starting today, create amongst your people a climate of inspiration. Sit them down if necessary, spell out the biggest problem facing the department and ask for inspired ideas on how to solve that problem. Rank the ideas and shortlist three. Now ask your team to evaluate each shortlisted idea. There is one condition. The implementation of the idea must be the responsibility of an individual or group of individuals within the team. They must be prepared to commit to that responsibility. If you need help to discover some inspired ideas, call in a consultant or your personnel person.

REMEMBER

You'll never find a SUPERBOSS lacking in inspiration.

Integrity

What price integrity when the fittest must survive and the killer instinct prevails? Can you reach the top and still have integrity?

There is a language among managers – 'back-stabbing', 'dropping someone in the mire', 'covering one's tracks', 'turning into a boot-licker', 'running with the hare and hunting with the hounds', 'becoming a sacrificial lamb', 'entering the rat race', or 'being out for blood'.

It is the language of the jungle. It is the language of frightened people who manage in the dark, beneath the surface of honesty, respectability and principle. It is the language of an organisation lacking in integrity. It is the language where fairness and justice is seen not to prevail.

In the jungle the rules are never clear. You have to make them up as you go along in order to survive. The Superboss refuses to enter this jungle. He exudes integrity. Everyone will know that he is a man of principle, totally honest. You will never find the Superboss playing games with his or her people's livelihoods.

The Superboss will refuse to join in any form of jungle fighting, even if it means putting his job on the line. The Superboss will always seek to make, and obtain, fair and objective decisions. The rules by which he manages will always be clear to the people in his organisation. The Superboss will have no select band of 'blue-eyed boys' or mercenary 'jungle fighters'. You will never find the Superboss 'going for someone's throat' or 'trying to creep in through the back door'.

The Superboss doesn't spy on his people, nor does he try to catch them out. The Superboss doesn't go on witch hunts or look for scapegoats.

The Superboss knows that profit is best achieved when employees and customers alike respect a company for its integrity. That integrity will be reflected in its management and leadership. Integrity is the basis of his credibility throughout the organisation.

ACTION TODAY

Do you pride yourself on your integrity? If not, why not? Look at the managers in your company, those who work for you, those who are your bosses, those elsewhere. How many visibly demonstrate a high degree of integrity? Put yourself at the top of the list and lead the way.

REMEMBER

The integrity of a SUPERBOSS should be beyond question.

Interest

To profit through people you must be interested in people

People can be difficult and you can lose interest in them rapidly. Some managers are much more interested in machines, financial figures, production plans, developing new products, or attending sales conferences overseas. Some managers are not at all interested in their people. Some managers will devote more than 80 per cent of their time to these non-people-oriented activities.

If you are not interested in your people, genuinely interested, then they certainly won't be interested in you and the company.

The Superboss shows an interest in all his people. He'll show an interest in Maureen Halman's new grandchild, in Stan Hunter's recent golfing vacation, in Rosella Flora's aerobics class. He'll approach the tattooed Ossie Brett and discuss heavy-metal with him before obtaining Marilyn Fields' opinion about the new Italian restaurant she went to with her boyfriend over the weekend.

And the Superboss will take an interest in what's happening on the production line, asking Bernie Britz about the new computer-controlled lathe before asking Bernie to give him a demonstration.

Then he'll wander up to Technical Services to chat to the company's new graduate trainees Jill Freeman and Gary Porter about their initial impression of the company.

To take an interest in his people the Superboss will spend more than 80 per cent of his time on people-related activities, walking the patch, chatting to them, reviewing progress, taking an interest in their training, in their careers, in their working conditions, in their problems, in everything that has an impact on their effectiveness and satisfaction at work.

He knows that interest is two-way. If he's interested in them, and shows it, more than likely they will reciprocate.

ACTION TODAY

Take a walk around your department. Show an interest in what your people are doing; casually chat to them about how things are. Don't pry into their private lives, but do take an interest in their families, in their social lives, in their sport.

Discipline yourself to go out and about, taking an interest, at least four times a week. Encourage other people to be interested too in what's going on in your area. Invite the Personnel Manager to walk around with you, or the Divisional Director or Chief Executive.

You'll be surprised how people respond to interest.

REMEMBER

The last thing the SUPERBOSS pursues is self-interest.

Involvement

The more you involve the less likely the revolt

Involvement concerns cohesion and contribution. Lack of involvement will lead to divisiveness and retribution.

Involvement is the process of securing commitment. If you are involved, you will contribute and you will commit. If you are involved, you will identify with the team's goals, you will want to share in the success.

Involvement requires time, and the Superboss takes time to involve his people. It requires a tremendous effort because other people can be so frustrating at times. They can appear to slow you down and you will want to ignore them and not involve them. But nowadays people will revolt if you don't involve them. You might not see the rebellion to begin with, it might fester under the surface for a long time. But in the end, if you don't involve them they will revolt and you won't be there. They will.

The Superboss involves his people in whatever he can, mostly in matters concerning them directly, whether it be a new factory layout, the purchase of a new type of truck or methods of improving efficiency. In involving others he doesn't abdicate his responsibilities. They know and he knows that the final decision will always be his. He will have to take responsibility for it. By involving his people the decision is more likely to be right. By involving his people he secures their commitment to the implementation of that decision. Instead of resisting the introduction of new technology they will demand it, if they've been involved in the evaluation studies.

The Superboss not only involves his people in the company's problems, he involves himself in their problems. He encourages them to bring their problems to him. He involves himself in trying to sort them out, in trying to help.

The Superboss loves being involved and having all his people involved whether it be at the front line or elsewhere.

ACTION TODAY

Write down the three most important projects you are involved with at the moment. Against each project list the names of those involved.

Now list the people, or the groups of people, who will be affected by that project.

Is a representative cross-section of people from this latter list involved in each project?

If the answer is no, involve them today before it's too late.

REMEMBER

You cannot be a member of the SUPERBOSS's team without being involved.

Joining in

The manager who joins in is never left behind

How can you understand if you don't join in? How can you appreciate the problem of emptying sludge tanks if you've never emptied them yourself? If you have, you might be a little more sympathetic to a request for improved protective gear.

Progressive companies make it the rule that senior executives and managers undertake front-line duties at least three times a year.

The Superboss joins in not only because he wants to help, but because he wants to understand. Nobody expects a Superboss to type, or program computer systems, but they do expect him to join in and load pallets when they're short of staff and there's an urgent job; they do expect him to pick up a ringing telephone and answer when the whole office is rushed off its feet; they do expect him to serve in the shop when they're one short at the counter for a while.

There can be no set pattern to joining in. Some Superbosses might go down at the end of every shift to help clear up so everyone can get away on time. Others might join in when there's a rush order to be dispatched. Others might join in on a regular basis because they want to understand what's going on in the factory. Others automatically join in to help their staff resolve a serious problem. Others just join in for the sheer fun of it.

In joining in nobody expects the Superboss to do more than he's capable of.

The Superboss does not let union demarcation lines prevent him from joining in. He'll explain, he'll discuss it with the union, but he'll insist he must join in. It's not to take his people's jobs away from them, far from it. It's to help understand their jobs, it's to help his people. It will make them feel important because the Superboss will never be able to do as good a job as them.

ACTION TODAY

Wander round your department and just join in, help push that trolley they're struggling with, pick up a bin and empty it when you're chatting to the cleaners: 'I hope you don't mind me helping'. Open a few envelopes in the mail room. Ask the training manager whether you can join in his next management course. Sit with the transport drivers. Take a van out with one of them and perhaps drive it for a few miles to give the driver a rest. Join in wherever you can today! They'll respect you for it.

REMEMBER

The SUPERBOSS joins in because he wants to help and he wants to understand.

Judgement

Management prejudice is the biggest threat to fair and objective judgement

Prejudice within management is a disease. Not only racial, religious, sexual or even status prejudice, but the way managers make prejudicial decisions about people.

Managers allow many things to cloud their judgement. It might be the primary coloured shirts Roland Cribbs wears, or Frank Harper's unfortunate obesity. It might be that Eddie Romain has a clipped staccato-like accent, or that Angie Solloway breeds dogs in her spare time. Often it's more subtle than that. 'There were problems with Sylvan Shaloma a few years ago'. You're not sure what the problems were, but you're left with a doubt.

Managers allow emotions to affect their judgement, or opinions passed on by other people. Someone will say: 'I wouldn't even consider Jason Kenny for that post, he's bloody useless'. Jason Kenny is ruled out before a fair and objective judgement can be made about him.

Prejudice comes in all shapes and colours. There can be prejudice against unions ('they'll find fault in everything'); or against people from Personnel ('a lot of useless do-gooders'); or against people from the Maudelonde Factory down the road ('they're a bunch of lazy good-for-nothings').

Prejudice at best is based on half-baked half-truths, and at worst on blind assumptions and total ignorance. Prejudice often occurs because people don't belong to the 'clan'.

The Superboss tries hard to eliminate any pressing prejudicial noise when having to make judgements about people. Whatever the issue (choosing a supplier, selecting a promotion candidate, making a disciplinary decision) he will always try to give a person a fair hearing. He will always try to collect as much factual evidence as possible and be objective in analysing his findings and making a judgement as to what is best for the company and its people. He will try to eliminate subjective influences ('Jennie Lester went to the same school as me') and he will never breach his own very strict moral and ethical code.

The Superboss prides himself on his fair and objective judgement and his people respect him for it.

ACTION TODAY

Re-examine the last important people decision you made (whether a promotion, a selection or a disciplinary action). Check through all your thought processes. Note the key factors that influenced your decision, any doubts you had, for example resulting from insufficient information, or whether or not you believed a statement. Now put your hand on your heart and say to yourself: 'That was the very best decision I would have made, my judgement was fair and wholly objective, and I did not allow any prejudice to sway me'.

Say that every time you make a judgement about anyone (boss, subordinate, supplier or colleague).

REMEMBER

The judgement of a SUPERBOSS will never be clouded by a flow of alcohol and excellent food. Nor by a smiling face with inviting eyes.

Know what you're talking about

What you say is not necessarily a reflection of what you know

Everybody is an expert on how to run the company. Or so it seems when they're telling you what the Directors should be doing. Not that they've ever carried any responsibility for running the company, nor have they had to make the tough decisions required at the top.

The same applies to personnel issues. Everyone knows better than Personnel on the subject of pay policy, or staffing levels.

These people are the five-second experts. They form strongly held opinions after five seconds' consideration of issues that fall into other people's areas of expertise. You'll hear them holding forth about the company's atrocious advertising, about the poor attitudes of the employees, about why the company should do this or that.

The Superboss listens quietly to the real experts and doesn't pretend he's one. He might ask a question or two for clarification, but he believes it's a mark of disrespect to imply to the Advertising Manager that he knows better how to produce advertisements.

When the Superboss makes a statement or expresses an opinion, he knows what he's talking about. He will have gathered the facts previously. He will have taken immense care in analysing the data and drawing conclusions. If he forms an opinion, it will be as a result of that careful study. You will never hear the Superboss rushing around telling his colleagues, 'David Grinstead was a bloody fool to cut expenditure back on that Italian project. Now look what's happened.'

Only the five-second expert would dare apply hindsight on what David Grinstead should have done three months ago. The Superboss wasn't in his shoes, or anywhere near them, so he'll refuse to give an opinion because he would not know what he's talking about.

The Superboss has learnt by observing others that those who tend to talk the most are those who know the least.

ACTION TODAY

Discipline yourself to hold back on the opinions you express, the statements you make. Always ask yourself, 'Do I really know what I'm talking about?'

If not, keep quiet. Let the experts do the talking.

REMEMBER

To become a SUPERBOSS you must know what you're talking about.

Know your people

If you don't know your people, you know nothing

There are many managers who don't know their people. It's unforgivable. They think they know. Nobody will ever own up to not knowing his or her people, mainly because they don't know they don't know.

What they do know is the surface behaviour of their people, the external face of each person. They will see the fronts people put up. But they will see no more. They won't know what lies under that cosmetic smile. They won't know what those polite words hide. They will not know their people.

The Superboss does know. He gets under the surface. He breaks the ice gently by thawing out the start of any conversation, talking about minor unimportant things to begin with. He relaxes the person, is friendly, smiles a lot. He tries hard to put a person at his ease, to unfreeze the initial tension. Then, because he's interested, he begins to know the person by asking unbiased questions about what's going on, how he or she feels about this or that, what his or her concerns are. The Superboss doesn't frown if the person gives a stupid answer, or stutters, or is lost for words. He encourages the person to talk. The Superboss doesn't interrupt with opinions, doesn't automatically disagree. He waits until the other person finishes because he respects that that person has something important to say, whatever it is.

In that way the Superboss learns to know his people. They will feel he understands, because he's given them time and he's genuinely interested in them. They will feel confident that when a problem arises they can take it to him, because he cares and he knows. And that's enough for them.

ACTION TODAY

Be honest with yourself. Do you really know your people? How often do you call up an individual for a free-ranging informal chat? Ask your secretary to arrange for you to spend an hour individually with a cross-section of your people over the next four weeks (whether or not they report to you). Explain that it is for an informal chat, just to see how things are going.

Once in a while a person will look blank and tell you little, but most times they'll tell you a lot. You'll know them much better.

REMEMBER

Frequently the SUPERBOSS knows more about his people than they know about themselves.

Leadership

What is the difference between a manager and a leader?

If you don't know the answer to that question, you're not a leader.

The saddest thing that has happened over recent decades is that many managers have lost their leadership skills. (Of course, many never had any in the first place.)

The ever-increasing complexities of the modern business environment with its burgeoning corporate bureaucracies and incessant change has led to a pitiful neglect in developing and training first-class leaders. Too many managers see their task as administration, pushing paper around, or progress chasing this and that. Leadership is lost as the Personnel experts and centralists at Head Office take over.

The Superboss is a leader. He takes command. He knows what he has to achieve and he's out there in front with his team achieving it. Leadership is helping your company stay ahead of the competition. It is obtaining the co-operation, consent and commitment of your team to go to the ends of the earth to achieve your objective. It is persuading people to accept your authority to make critical decisions. The Superboss does it by inspiration, by example, by sound judgement. He does it by using all the practices mentioned in this book.

The Superboss is also brave enough to lead the way in making painful decisions. He never shies away from a difficult issue or task. He never shies away from his people if an unpopular decision has to be made. He consults them as he goes. He explains the reasons for his decisions and leads them from there.

The Superboss believes in his people, has conviction, has control. And he has command. He knows where he's going and he leads his people there, because they share that self-same conviction, that self-same belief and they accept his authority, his command, his leadership.

ACTION TODAY

Unless you've been on one in the last year, put yourself on a leadership training course. Ring the Training Manager and do it today! If you're Chief Executive, do the same. (You can go to Geneva so that no one will notice.)

Every manager needs leadership training at least once a year.

REMEMBER

Being a SUPERBOSS is synonymous with being a great leader.

Learning

Once you stop learning you're dead, or at least you appear that way to your subordinates

One of the worst managers I ever met thought he knew everything. He was very convincing. In fact he almost convinced me he was the world's leading expert on everything.

He thought he knew why his staff were unhappy. (He didn't ask them because he thought he knew better.) He addressed the wrong problem. He paid them more because one or two had moaned about money and that was easy to understand. And when they started resigning and leaving the company he still didn't learn. So he was removed from his job and he still has to learn why.

All they wanted was a manager who was prepared to learn about what they thought; learn about their ideas for making administration, supply, distribution and operational procedures more efficient. They were desperate to help the company improve; to do so would help them maintain their professional pride in doing an excellent job. He didn't see it that way. Their job was to do their job, not suggest improvements. That was his job. He knew best, he was the boss, he had nothing to learn from them. In fact they should be learning from him (after all he was always giving them lectures).

The Superboss learns a little every day from the people who know best, the people on the job. He learns from them how to put things right, how to make improvements. He learns about their problems and how he can help. He learns from his own mistakes and those of his team. He respects the knowledge, the experience, the skills, the wisdom of the people around him and draws from it in helping the team perform outstandingly.

The Superboss learns from everyone – his people, his boss, his colleagues, Personnel and other specialists. He learns from employee representatives, unions and anyone who is prepared to give genuine honest advice.

The Superboss never stops learning, never stops wanting to learn.

ACTION TODAY

What have you learnt today? Write it down. If you can't, you've learnt nothing and you're no better a person than you were yesterday, or probably the day before, or last year.

Having written it down, annotate each item of learning with the name of the 'teacher', whether that person be a subordinate, colleague, employee representative or your boss. Then go and see the 'teacher' and say how much you appreciated his or her advice, say you found it helpful and learnt something new as a result.

REMEMBER

Becoming a SUPERBOSS never happens by chance, you have to learn to become one.

Listening

Having learnt to talk, who learns to listen?

People who don't listen are a constant source of irritation. Having listened to them drone on for ten minutes you try to say something and before you complete your sentence they're off again, regardless of what you've tried to say. At meetings they rustle through papers, yawn, scratch their noses, wipe their spectacles and chat idly to the person next to them when someone else is talking. If the subject interests them they still don't listen, but sit on the edge of their seats eager to interrupt and interject irrespective of what the last person said. For these people the most important thing in the world is telling other people what they think. Discovering what others think has very low priority in their way of life.

The Superboss is a keen listener. He is humble enough to know that he has much to learn from what others say. In fact he knows that just by listening when someone comes to him with a problem, perhaps by asking the occasional question, the person will often find the solution to his or her problem.

The Superboss listens attentively to his team and goes out of his way to do so, creating frequent opportunities to hear what they have to say, to take into account their views, understand their problems. He lets them have their say first, not commenting until he's clear about their position.

The Superboss, although a superb listener, knows how to handle 'wafflers', discreetly drawing their disconnected and extended monologues to a close with a degree of diplomacy the speaker is probably oblivious to.

The Superboss knows that listening is a skill requiring great powers of stamina, self-control, concentration and understanding. But he knows that on most occasions listening is more productive than talking.

But listening is not enough. For the Superboss listening means taking action on what he hears. It is not enough to collect words. He needs to ensure that something happens as a result of listening to others. Too often he has heard people say 'I raised that issue with the boss three months ago and nothing's happened'. That's not the Superboss. He might not always agree with what he hears, but he'll always do something about it.

ACTION TODAY

Walk round your patch today and ask: 'How are things going?' and listen. And if you receive a hesitant non-committal distant reply probe a little deeper. For example: 'How do you find this new computerised supply system?' and listen. You'll learn a lot.

If someone walks in and says: 'Boss, I've got a problem with the new set up in Zone G', just listen. Within five minutes he or she will be telling you the solution, and it'll probably be a better one than you would have suggested had you not listened.

ACTION TOMORROW

Discipline yourself to take notes when listening to people and ensure that action points are recorded.

Then follow through and take action.

REMEMBER

The SUPERBOSS has learnt to listen, and listens to learn.

Maintaining face

The preservation of face is the highest priority in maintaining an effective relationship

We can all lose face. Perhaps it's when someone scowls at us, swears at us, makes us feel silly or makes a fool of us.

Losing face often comes from unintentional behaviour by the other person. It could be an abrupt end to a telephone call, or a bored look, or not looking you in the eyes. (It's very important to look someone in the eyes.)

No one wants to feel small. Everyone has an inner dignity which he or she wishes to preserve; a dignity based on pride and the awareness that if I am employed by this organisation I must have some value and importance to it.

Everyone has to go home after work and face a wife, husband, partner, child or a friend. At home you want to be proud about your work. The last thing you want is to have your tail between your legs because you've lost face amongst your colleagues, or because someone has slighted you and made you feel small, unwanted, unimportant.

Certain people can brazen it out, maintain a brave face, but for most there will be a deep-down hurt with a sense of rejection and unimportance.

The Superboss is sensitive to people's inner dignity, to their pride. Maintaining face is of the highest priority in preserving his relationship with every person around him. He takes care not to slight anyone, not to make them feel bad. He does his best to let others know that they are as important to the organisation as everyone else.

When difficult situations arise, when the facts of poor behaviour or poor performance have to be faced, the Superboss does it with dignity, with the object of maintaining face. 'Look Richard you might not like what I'm going to say, but I want to help you. The problem is, the way you're acting at the moment makes it difficult for everyone. You're often late, your attitude to your colleagues and the customers is indifferent, to say the least. What's more, you're just not coping with your workload. Now let's talk about how we can tackle these problems . . .' The Superboss wants to help, help maintain face.

ACTION TODAY

Every time you meet someone today put yourself in their shoes. Ask yourself how he or she reacts when you speak, when you look at them. How would you feel if someone spoke to you like that, looked at you like that? Discipline yourself always to be conscious and aware of what impact you're having on the other person. He or she is employed by the company, he or she is important. Reflect it in the way you face that person.

REMEMBER

By helping people maintain face the SUPERBOSS helps people preserve their inner dignity and self-esteem.

Managing people

Managing people successfully is your greatest professional challenge

It is blatantly obvious that only trained, qualified and experienced pilots will be put in command of an aeroplane.

Human beings display a different order of complexity from an aeroplane. But they are complex all the same.

Time after time organisations appoint to management and supervisory positions people with negligible experience, skills, training, or potential for the complex task of commanding people.

Would you put an untrained, unqualified person in command of an aircraft? Then why put one in command of people?

The Superboss is a trained and qualified expert in managing people successfully. He will have attended management training courses and benefited greatly from them. If he hasn't had the chance he will have trained himself, seizing any opportunity to learn more about management, to improve his skills in this vital task. The Superboss will be both a management expert and a management enthusiast. Every scrap of experience he will question and learn from. Even as a junior he'll have learned from the way his various bosses managed him, and whether or not that affected his motivation and performance.

The Superboss will always debate managerial excellence with other management enthusiasts, even staying up to midnight to discuss the complexities of managing a dynamic group of people.

What's more the Superboss wouldn't dream of appointing anyone to a management position without having first given that person some relevant training and development, and then carefully monitoring progress and helping the new manager with feedback and counsel.

The Superboss, from all his experience, will evolve his own philosophy of management, his own set of beliefs of what constitutes managerial excellence. He'll develop his own style of management.

The Superboss knows that the process of managing others successfully is difficult and requires an immense amount of time and a high degree of devotion. It requires a great investment, both personally and by the company in management training and development.

ACTION TODAY

Devote some time this evening to writing a short paper (no more than three sides) on what you believe is involved in managing people successfully. Tomorrow circulate the paper to one or two of your colleagues (assuming they're managers), convene a lunchtime session and debate managerial excellence with them. You'll be surprised at the ideas that come up and what you'll learn.

REMEMBER

The results a SUPERBOSS achieves are those he manages to achieve.

Managing time

Time is a scarce and valuable resource which has to be managed effectively to achieve results

Managers are paid for the efficient use of their time. Their contribution is a direct result of how they use it, how they prioritise it.

The Superboss doesn't let the constant stream of extraneous events, demands, telephone calls and mail dictate the use of his time. He takes control of his time and plans it carefully.

The Superboss doesn't overload his diary with too many meetings, or too many trips. The Superboss doesn't allow others to manipulate his diary, nor overrule what he has scheduled for it. The Superboss will never allow his time to be at the beck and call of his boss.

Managers who are kept running at the behest of their bosses are the worst type. Sometimes even bosses have to wait; normally they understand. The Superboss, for example, would not delay or cancel an interview just because his boss called an urgent meeting.

However, the Superboss plans for a fair amount of 'slack' in his diary so that he can deal with contingencies. He learns how often his boss is likely to place an urgent demand on him, and plans his time accordingly. His people will learn that the Superboss allocates an hour of free time in his diary at 9.00 am and 2.00 pm each day and that's the best time to phone him or see him for five minutes.

The Superboss also plans far in advance, slotting into his diary up to a year ahead appraisal dates, formal briefing sessions, progress reviews and, of course, vacations. The last thing he'll do is allow his secretary to fill his diary and then find that not only does he have to cancel meetings when urgent problems arise, but also that he has allocated no time for appraisals, briefing sessions and progress reviews.

The priorities a Superboss allocates to his time are a reflection of what he really values at work.

ACTION TODAY

Check your diary against the following 'test' criteria:

1 Do you have at least 40 per cent blank time to deal with matters arising?
2 Do you have the performance appraisals of your team planned twelve months ahead?
3 Have you set aside time for 'walking the patch'?
4 Are your regular briefing sessions and progress reviews firmly slotted into your diary?
5 Have you set aside dates for your vacation?
6 Have you diplomatically explained to your boss and your people your approach to planning and managing your time?

If the answer to any of these questions is 'no,' plan accordingly and make the necessary changes.

REMEMBER

The SUPERBOSS plans his own time, rather than lets other people plan it for him.

Memos

Memos are no substitute for management

Memos are a dumb way of communicating. They tend to fall on deaf ears and are symptomatic of the lazy, inept, unthinking, can't be bothered manager.

I remember the memo from one of my colleagues which read: 'When you have five minutes could we discuss my previous memo on employee relations'. His office was ten yards along the corridor from mine and I saw him at least twice a day. He was always sending me memos like that. I never replied. I always went along to see him.

Many incompetent paranoiac managers write memos for insurance reasons, keeping vast files of 'I told you so' documents. But people rarely check back. How could you, with all those reams of paper? Throw them away!

The Superboss writes memos only as a last resort when he knows that face-to-face communication or a quick telephone call will not serve the purpose.

He'll never write memos to express opinions, to issue group reprimands, or to issue minor instructions. Furthermore the Superboss knows the difference between a memo, a letter, a formal request, a contract, a report, a discussion paper and a department notice.

The Superboss will react sharply to memo writers who try to earn glory points by copying everyone else on. 'Haven't I done a good job' memos. He'll take that person aside and explain that there's no glory in writing memos.

The Superboss knows that memos lead to documentary dermatitis and coronaries of the communications system. They lead to psycho-organisational disorders such as interdepartmental misunderstandings and demotivational malpractice. In short, inefficiency.

The Superboss prefers face-to-face, or ear-to-mouth communications, suffering 'white-outs' when confronted with too much paper.

ACTION TODAY

Ask your secretary to destroy all memos written or received by you during the last five years.

ACTION TOMORROW

Don't write any memos, nor any replies. Every time you're tempted to write a memo eat an apple and see if you can identify a better way of carrying out that communication – wait for your next team meeting, pick up a telephone, or go and see the person concerned.

REMEMBER

Nobody becomes a SUPERBOSS because of his or her memos.

Mistakes

The more mistakes a manager admits the more likely he or she is to be successful

Weak managers see admitting mistakes as a sign of weakness, an admission of failure, an exposure of their own inadequacies. Admitting mistakes makes them feel vulnerable. They worry about loss of credibility in the eyes of their subordinates, their colleagues and, what is worse, their bosses. They fear they will be passed over for promotion, will receive no merit increase. They fear that others will exploit their mistakes, point fingers at them, show them up.

So weak managers cover up their mistakes. They hide them and hope no one will notice. If someone accuses them of making a mistake they become defensive, difficult to pin down. They avoid the subject.

In covering up mistakes the weak managers delude themselves and pass over opportunities for improvement.

Some managers have nothing else to do but wait for other people to make mistakes. Then they're in their element. They point out the mistakes, demand 'blood' and hover like vultures waiting for the next one to be made.

The Superboss gains strength from admitting mistakes. For a start he knows he can learn from his mistakes and learn from other people in discussing them. Furthermore, in admitting mistakes, he knows that there's little further action people can take. No boss can issue a written warning every time a mistake is made. The cry for 'blood' normally disappears as soon as someone is brave enough and big enough to admit the mistake.

The Superboss also knows how to manage other people's mistakes. The last thing he'll do is kick them for their mistakes, he doesn't manage that way. The first thing he'll do is help them learn from the mistake. That's mistake management.

In admitting and managing mistakes the Superboss facilitates remedial action and thus creates opportunities for improvement.

ACTION TODAY

This will be an acid test to see if you're a Superboss. Write down five mistakes you've made in the last twelve months. (If you haven't made any you should be Chief Executive by now and running the most profitable operation in the country.)

Prioritise the mistakes and then write down the remedial action you took and what you learnt.

If you're brave enough (and this is not compulsory) ask your boss to help you by indicating some of the mistakes you've made this last year. See how your boss's list compares with your own. You might be surprised and learn from it!

REMEMBER

The SUPERBOSS has probably made many more mistakes than you. That's why he's a SUPERBOSS.

Motivation

Money, whips and magic wands are useless motivational aids in management

If money were the source of all motivation then we would all be on piece-work schemes. If motivation could be simplified into a simple XYZ theory then we would all be happy. In reality the ability to motivate others derives from the ability to motivate yourself.

And that's where the Superboss starts. He knows that if he is not motivated himself, there's no likelihood his people will be. With no boss at his back the Superboss will work hard at weekends to grow beautiful roses. That's self-motivation.

The Superboss will be self-motivated to achieve results that are critical for the company. The actual process of achieving something has an intrinsic satisfaction for him. Pay will not motivate him, although he'll see it as a useful barometer of success. The Superboss will be turned neither on nor off by threats, exhortation or cajolery. He'll keep his eye on the target and that will be the source of his motivation.

Encouragement and support from his boss will help him along and make him feel good at times. It will keep him going when he feels like giving up. But primarily the Superboss is self-motivated and will only become demotivated (albeit temporarily) if he's constantly held back or unfairly treated.

The Superboss is no different from his people, and he knows it. Their motivation derives from his. His motivation shows through in his enthusiasm for the task at hand, his excitement about the progress they are making, his support for his people. The Superboss will try very hard to eliminate demotivators such as poor pay, cramped working environment, inadequate tools, company politics, unsympathetic supervision and unfair practices. But in the end he knows that motivation is a positive attitude of mind which cannot be manipulated with money.

ACTION TODAY

To be anything like a Superboss you must have your own theory of
motivation and, what's more, you must be able to put it into practice.
Think about that theory today, check your practices. Ask yourself
what motivates you and then ask yourself why it should be any
different for your people.

Test your theories and practices on other people. You might learn
something about motivation.

REMEMBER

Self-motivation is the key for the SUPERBOSS.

Needs

No two people have the same needs, yet many managers assume they do

Needs. We all have them, especially at work. Besides equipment needs (tools etc.), we have environmental needs (toilets etc.) and social needs (someone to listen to our moans) as well as personal needs of all types. The need for more money, the need to be praised, the need to be recognised, the need to be consulted, the need to be challenged, the need to achieve something, the need for personal satisfaction and self-esteem. The need to get away from it all and do something different.

Needs. We all have them, but they are all different. You cannot sit in your 'ivory tower' and blindly assume that the thousand people in the organisation have the same needs.

The Superboss finds out the individual needs of his people – those who need to progress and be promoted; those who need a transfer because they need a change of scenery; those who need a new desk top computer; those who need talking to. He discovers their even more complex motivational needs – for frequent praise or encouragement, for the occasional ticking-off, or to be left alone to do the job.

The Superboss also makes sure the team knows his needs: for performance, for high standards, for close consultation and communication, for honesty, for openness and straight talking, for people to admit their mistakes before he finds out. The Superboss needs all that and much more. He makes it clear he needs complete commitment and dedication to the task. He needs loyalty to the team and to the company. And to him.

Ultimately the Superboss needs what the company needs: results!

ACTION TODAY

Phone the Personnel Manager and ask him or her to sit down with you and complete a needs analysis for every member of your team. Look at training needs, development needs, motivational needs, environmental needs, physical needs, personal needs and any other needs you can think of.

Having identified all of them, categorise them into those needs which have the most immediate impact on profit and on the person.

Then do something about those priority needs. Take action. Telephone the person and discuss the observed needs with him or her. Once agreed take action to meet the need. Book the training course, buy the new desk, give more praise. The business needs it, he or she needs it, and you need to do it.

REMEMBER

People need a SUPERBOSS to really understand their needs.

Objectives

Management By Objectives (MBO) was invented in the 1950s – right or wrong?

Wrong! Management by objectives was invented by Alexander the Great in 340 BC at the tender age of 15. He managed to take a flying expedition to the North of Greece, conquer the rebels and rename their city Alexandropolis. That was his first objective. Then came Asia Minor.

Management terminology becomes a little confused when it tries to differentiate between objectives, goals, purpose, aims, targets, end-results, outcomes, standards, missions, strategies and plans of action, or even 'critical success factors'.

We'll stick with objectives here and define them as the specific contribution required of a manager. In other words, the key results the person is accountable for achieving. For a Chief Executive the key results will probably include profit, revenue growth, market share and effective employee relations. Each objective, each key result will need a specific measure of achievement, quantitative or qualitative.

A cascade of subsidiary objectives will flow from those of the Chief Executive.

The Superboss will know exactly what his subset of contribution objectives are. They won't be a long list of thirty, but probably between three to eight. They will be specific and directly geared to the company's strategic objectives. He'll constantly have them in mind when leading his team.

They don't necessarily need to be written down, although it sometimes helps. The Superboss and his team will be wholly clear about these objectives and especially about their measures of achievement. They will be his objectives and nobody else's. He'll have sole accountability for achieving them. Furthermore he'll know that the company's future success is critically dependent on their achievement.

For the Superboss clear objectives are vitally important, he couldn't manage without them.

ACTION TODAY

Examine your objectives and make sure you are totally clear about them. Check with your team. If you don't have any objectives, produce some immediately. Write down what you think they are and show your boss. Get him or her to agree, or modify them as a result of the discussion.

You must have objectives, it's what the company requires of you. You must be clear about them. So must your team. Check today.

ACTION NEXT WEEK

Review your objectives at your next team meeting.

REMEMBER

No SUPERBOSS can manage without clear-cut objectives.

Open door

There's only one interpretation of an open-door policy: any employee can walk through that door when it's open (which it frequently is)

An open-door policy doesn't mean your door is open all the time. It doesn't mean that only your immediate subordinates can call in when it's open.

It means that anyone in your company, division, department or section can come and see you when that door's open. There will be no secretary barring entry or creating obstacles if a junior tries to see you for five minutes.

When his door is open the Superboss will give a warm welcome to whoever wants to see him, whatever the issue. If the Superboss doesn't want to see anyone, he'll close the door. If the Superboss is in a confidential meeting, he'll close the door. If he wants to make a few telephone calls or quietly go through some urgent papers, he'll close the door.

The Superboss however will try to keep his door open as much as possible. He'll forbid his secretary to 'close off' more than 60 per cent of his diary. He'll keep the 40 per cent free for the open door or for walking the patch. When he's sitting at his desk with an open door he'll use the time profitably by going through the mail, catching up with some of the reading, or making one or two brief telephone calls. If Tina Bailey from Accounts pokes her head round the door, he'll welcome her in with a wave of the arm and give her a couple of minutes.

Although the Superboss keeps his door open frequently, he'll do nothing to undermine the authority of his immediate subordinates. There will be no problem because his immediate team encourage their more junior staff to call in and see the Superboss occasionally to advise him of progress, to discuss issues and problems with him.

In the view of the Superboss and his team visibility up, down and across the organisation is welcomed and does not interfere with hierarchical accountability.

ACTION TODAY

Open your door today for at least two hours. Instruct your secretary not to object to anyone coming in. If no one comes in, it's because you're not a Superboss and people are not used to it. In which case you'd better start spreading the message that your door's open and you mean it. Call up one or two people (other than your immediate subordinates) for a chat. Let them and others know that your door's frequently open.

REMEMBER

For a SUPERBOSS an open door is the opposite of a closed mind.

Open mind

The more open your mind the more opportunities open up for you to seize

Historical evidence suggests that many people become victims of their own success. Having found a formula to reach the top they become wholly resistant to suggestions that there might be other formulae that could be even more successful.

These people become trapped in rigid thinking patterns which ultimately limit their capability. They become self-righteous and presume to know all the answers, dismissing suggestions from less experienced people. All this is based on one of the most dangerous assumptions around: 'Because it worked for me in the past, it will work for me in the future'.

Keeping an open mind is one of the Superboss's biggest challenges. He is always open to the possibility that his way might not be the best way, that his people have better ideas about solving a problem than he does.

Keeping an open mind means never jumping to conclusions. It means giving every single individual in the team an opportunity to have their say. It means never making a decision before weighing up all the arguments.

The Superboss is open to the possibility that there are other possibilities. There is the possibility that he could be wrong in assessing Mark Richie's poor performance. There is the possibility that Michelle Stratton could have been right that customer service has been deteriorating despite a reduction in complaints.

By keeping an open mind the Superboss opens up so many possibilities to become even more successful.

ACTION TODAY

Find someone in your team who is prepared to be brutally honest with you. Persuade him (or her) to challenge your most cherished assumptions – e.g. that performance-related pay is effective, that Cheryl Headington is the best consultant around, that morale is excellent in West Bay.

ACTION TOMORROW

Having identified the assumptions which need verification gather your team together and discuss them with them. Be open to the possibility that you might have to change your position on some of these points.

REMEMBER

The wisdom of a SUPERBOSS springs from an open mind.

Open up

The manager who opens up is the manager who opens the way to finding the solution

The Superboss opens up to his people, to his boss, to his colleagues, to his immediate team.

He knows that the more he 'closes up', the less people will trust him. The Superboss likes to open up problems, rather than push them below the surface. Often the problem is no more than a bad feeling he has about something or somebody.

If he feels unhappy about the way Annette Marks has been approaching her work, he'll open up and tell her just that. 'I want to be open and honest with you, Annette. I feel unhappy about the way things are going at the moment'. He'll try to explain why.

If he's disappointed about the lack of progress in installing a new wash unit in Bay 3, he'll open up and tell his team.

The process of opening up to his people reveals the Superboss's emotions. It shows that when it comes to emotion and intellect, he's not all intellect; that when it comes to heart and mind he's not all mind. By revealing his feelings the Superboss opens up his heart, and shows some emotion.

He opens up not to moan, not to undermine his people's confidence in him, not to disillusion them. He opens up because he wants to help his people and also he feels he owes it to them to let them know how he thinks and feels.

The Superboss also knows that if he opens up to his people, tells them how he feels, it's more likely they will open up to him.

By opening up the Superboss accesses problems quickly and resolves them.

ACTION TODAY

Set aside half an hour at coffee time and call in a couple of your team. Open up to them about your concerns, about one or two problems that are worrying you, about how you feel projects are progressing. Seek their advice and help.

Encourage them to open up on how they feel about specific points.

Your relationship with them will improve and it's possible you'll open your way to solving that nagging problem.

REMEMBER

Open up to a SUPERBOSS and he'll open up ways to help you.

Opportunities

Opportunities, opportunities, opportunities! Why do so many managers miss them?

Life is full of opportunities, that's what makes it so exciting. Don't blink now, you might be missing one!

Life at work is full of opportunities, no matter how good, how bad your company. Even in the perfect company dynamic change creates opportunity.

Managers miss opportunities because they're blind or, to be fair, they have not trained themselves to look for them. Vertical tracks do not lead to opportunities, and when you've followed them all your career the process of looking laterally for opportunities does not come easily.

The Superboss seizes an opportunity a day – an opportunity to motivate a junior supervisor by asking him or her to represent the company at a conference in Geneva; the opportunity to slash the distribution budget by replanning delivery schedules and reducing transport costs; the opportunity to bring his team together for a game of golf on Friday afternoon; the opportunity to meet Rob Hadon at Redland's and regain their business.

The Superboss knows that the best way to identify and seize opportunities is not to let the 'management routines' start managing him. Routines are ruts which lead to predictable results. Routines are the antithesis of entrepreneurial thinking.

Large unwieldy organisations, like dinosaurs, eventually die because they develop rigidly bureaucratic routines and régimes which stifle the entrepreneurial quest for opportunities and initiative, let alone survival.

The Superboss can beat a dinosaur any day in making a profit, in encouraging his people to seize opportunities, be creative and make progress. It's what makes working with a Superboss so exciting.

ACTION TODAY

Look at your diary, at your mail, at all those boring events you have planned for today. Look again and immerse yourself, even wallow, in that mire of bureaucracy and imminent committee meetings. Think only of the routines, the ruts and the boring bits.

Now think of green fields, flowers, rivers and distant mountains. The next thought that comes into your head should be an opportunity.

If it isn't, think again. And if that doesn't work, think again (always thinking of the boring bits first, then the green fields, the flowers, the rivers and the distant mountains).

Eventually you will think of an opportunity to do something special for your company and your team.

REMEMBER

The opportunity for you to become a SUPERBOSS exists right now. (Yes! This very minute.)

Overview

An inside view should always be balanced with an overview

When the rush is on, when the pressure mounts, it's not easy to step back and take an overview. But it is vital.

The manager under pressure will always have only a limited view. He'll see the surface problems and arrive at surface solutions. If the engineers have stopped work, if the production line is at a halt for the third time this week, if there's an irate customer on the line complaining about late delivery, if the Chairman is demanding to see him to explain what's going on, and if poor Tenny Kai wants to see him on a personal matter, then the last thing the typical manager might think about is taking an overview.

But the Superboss will. He'll step back and try to put the problems into perspective. By doing so he'll take control, rather than let events control him. That way he'll avoid a cosmetic solution. He'll decide to devote more time to getting to the heart of the engineers' problem. He'll decide to see that irate customer over lunch. Furthermore, he'll arrange to have a quiet half hour with the Chairman to chew the cud with him on the problems. And he won't forget poor Tenny Kai. He'll probably decide to see her first.

And at the weekend while playing golf the Superboss will take another overview, looking back at the events of the past week.

Once a month he'll sit down for some deep thinking. By taking frequent overviews the Superboss maintains a good perspective of the ever changing scene at his workplace.

ACTION TODAY

Mark into your diary three ten-minute overview sessions per week (you can use weekends). At each session think deeply about what's going on all around you. Jot down the key problems, your priorities, and then let your mind run free before forming an overview of the situation and deciding what new action you should take.

REMEMBER

In forming his overview the SUPERBOSS relates the company to people, the people to customers, and the customers to profit.

Pain

Management is as much about making painful decisions as about making decisions that please people

The worst managers never grasp nettles – they avoid the pain and the nettles grow.

Success doesn't come easily in management. For every satisfying decision you make, there always seems to be an equally painful one.

In a harsh competitive world you can do your best and still not do well enough, whether as a company, a manager or a junior employee.

The Superboss takes no delight in making painful decisions, but at least he will make them. Weaker managers will shy away from them.

The Superboss will only have to look at market trends and the downturn in figures to know that economies will be necessary. He will explore every conceivable way to avoid those economies adversely affecting his people. But in the end he will make the painful decision that jobs must go.

The Superboss will look at the way Tom Reuben has not quite been able to cope as Quality Control Manager, despite all the help, advice and encouragement given to him. In the end the Superboss will reluctantly conclude that Tom Reuben will have to be removed from the job.

It pains the Superboss to bring up the subject of poor performance with a loyal member of his team, but he will. It pains the Superboss to reject nine thoroughly good candidates for a key job (when the tenth was only marginally better), but he will. It pains the Superboss to raise a delicate issue with his own boss about the way he demotivates people with his brusque offensive manner, but he will.

In the end the Superboss will always take the pain rather than avoid the problem.

ACTION TODAY

Shut your door. Ask your secretary to leave you alone for half an hour. Make a critical review of all those difficult situations around you. Be honest. Is there one decision you're shying away from? Accept the pain and make the decision.

Review all the nettles you have grasped over recent times. Or is your garden perfect?

REMEMBER

The SUPERBOSS will not avoid a painful decision, but in implementing the decision he'll try to avoid the pain.

Participation

Participation is the key to commitment

The concept of participation confuses many managers. They agree with the principle but struggle with the practice. Many see it as workplace democracy, itself a controversial subject, and find it difficult to reconcile with the principles of accountability. A manager is not a manager unless he or she has sole accountability for making specified decisions.

The process of bringing people together round the table to participate in decision-making can be cumbersome and time-consuming. It does secure commitment, however, and is well worthwhile if all participants have the same underlying interest and can contribute some expertise towards making the decision. It will fail if there are conflicting selfish interests and the participants are not expert in the issue under consideration.

The Superboss makes decisions. He'll encourage interested parties to participate in the process, but if it's 51 of one and 49 of the other he'll make a decision and risk upsetting the 51.

But it's rarely like that. Wherever possible the Superboss will try to make his decision in accordance with the consensus view. However, when he has to go against that view he'll explain his reasons and try to help the participants understand.

To encourage participation on a regular basis the Superboss will share his thoughts with his people, will share his ideas, his enthusiasms and also his concerns. Equally he will try very hard to share their thoughts, their ideas, enthusiasms and concerns. Participation is a two-way process of giving, and giving of yourself. It is a continuing process that the Superboss will undertake informally every day. Participation is the antithesis of taking, of exploiting, of demanding, of imposition.

By participating and contributing to a decision employees are most likely to become committed to that decision.

Accountability, however, cannot be shared (otherwise you fire the whole group if things go wrong). No matter how much participation and sharing there is, the decision in the end will be that of the Superboss.

ACTION TODAY

Stroll around your area, share your thoughts with everyone you meet. Share with them your biggest concerns, your ideas about resolving some key problems. Invite them to share their ideas with you. Encourage them to participate in the resolution of some of the problems exposed and in some of the decisions that have to be made.

ACTION NEXT WEEK

Gather together for an informal meeting a cross-section of people in your area (representing all sections and levels).

Invite them to participate in a decision-making discussion about improvements at their place of work.

Listen carefully. Share with them your thoughts on the ideas they suggest. Try to obtain some consensus. Then make a decision and follow through.

Don't bypass your direct reports. Invite them to join in too. You might ask an employee relations specialist to chair the meeting.

REMEMBER

The SUPERBOSS recognises that the best decisions are those made by the people who have to implement them. It is these people he asks to participate in the decision-making process.

Pay

How you value people is reflected in the way you pay them

The Superboss has a simple philosophy about pay: 'To achieve the best results you must have the best people and to have the best people you must have the best pay'.

So the Superboss aims to pay people the best rate in the market place. In a competitive world you have to attract and keep the best. That means being at the top of the market when it comes to pay.

The last thing the Superboss wants to do is undervalue his people and make them feel bad. When people feel undervalued they perform badly.

Furthermore the Superboss pays everyone the best. He hates to differentiate on the basis of individual performance. Teamwork is the essence of his approach and to single out one or two people for extra rewards is anathema to him. He detests individual performance-related pay which he finds counter-productive, divisive and demotivating. If there are performance rewards he makes sure they are spread equally amongst the team.

On the issue of pay the Superboss takes action first. He doesn't wait for his people to come along and push for pay increases. He watches the market place and then fights his people's corner to ensure they are up with and possibly ahead of the leaders on pay.

In pushing for the highest pay the Superboss is always aware of the financial circumstances of the company, but if a choice has to be made on expenditure it will always be his people who come first. For him paying the best is an investment which bears long-term dividends.

It goes without saying that by paying the best he expects the best and anyone performing below their best he deals with appropriately (by training, counselling and occasionally firing poor performers).

ACTION TODAY

Review your people's pay. If they are not up with the market leaders currently then prepare a personal plan of action to put them there.

REMEMBER

The SUPERBOSS pays the best to gain the best.

People come first

People must come first in any organisation – they should be their most prized asset

Profit through people, not at the expense of them. Consider people as a prized asset, not as a variable cost.

This is a theme that runs consistently through this book. It is a key theme for the Superboss. People must come first, every time.

People come first in the allocation of the Superboss's time, first on his priority list.

That fact is so obvious but it's amazing that so many managers put other things first; they neglect to spend time with their people; neglect to take an interest in them; neglect to give attention to selecting them, to training them, to encouraging and supporting them, to helping them and to consulting them. They are managers who have more important things to do than fight battles on behalf of their people. You'll probably see these managers spending hours poring over new product designs, financial analyses or detailed project reports.

The Superboss knows that if he doesn't put his people first, they won't put him and the company first. Putting them first doesn't mean mouthing fine words like 'We are a people-caring company' or 'We have a listening management'. It means fine action. The Superboss puts his people first by fixing their car-parking problems, by sorting out the heating in the office, by giving priority to resolving a pay parity problem, by listening to their troubles and helping resolve them.

In deciding his priorities the Superboss always puts his people at the top of list. For him it is a priority to communicate with them, to train them, to listen to them and to motivate them.

ACTION TODAY

Examine how you allocate your time. Do you have a tendency to say to yourself: 'I haven't time to take a stroll around the department today, I must sort out this back-log of mail'? Do you prefer to get sucked into meetings with your boss rather than see Debbie Nash when she has a difficult problem to resolve?

How often do you initiate informal chats with people throughout your department? Would you prefer that some of those intractable people problems go away so that you could concentrate on completing that study on product reliability your boss called for?

Starting today, give high priority to the people issues. Take a stroll around your department, initiate a series of informal chats with some junior staff. Try to crack some of those intractable people problems ('Yes, I must confront John Peters rather than let him go on stirring up trouble').

REMEMBER

The SUPERBOSS never lets his people down, because he always puts them first.

Perceptions

Perceptions have a greater influence on people's attitudes and behaviour than facts

A politician was speaking recently on television. There had been some débacle in which the government had been accused of not listening to its own members. The politician kept saying, 'But we are a listening government'. The perception of the audience and the questioners was different. Every time he repeated the statement there was derisory laughter.

The company might say: 'We can't afford a pay increase', and present financial figures to demonstrate this. The perception might be otherwise. It might be that, if the company can afford to move to a new headquarters building, if it can afford an expensive new advertising campaign, if it can afford lavish entertainment for visiting dignitaries, then it can afford a pay increase.

A company might say: 'We are the people-caring company' and then assign the lowest budgetary priority to resolving a car-parking problem that has been bothering the staff for years.

Fine words cannot influence perception, only fine action.

The Superboss is very much concerned with the perceptions of his people. He's concerned that they see the company and his actions in the best light – a clear light which establishes genuine credibility for each policy, decision and communication.

Perceptions derive not from facts or words, but from people's actions. The Superboss knows that for perceptions to be favourable a manager must demonstrate total consistency between the words he utters and the decisions and actions he takes.

ACTION TODAY

List the three most important facts you have tried to convey to your people over the last four weeks.

Call your Personnel Manager and ask him or her to circulate and talk to your people, to check their perceptions of what they see as important.

Then compare notes. What is the degree of convergence between your perceptions and those of your people? You may be surprised.

REMEMBER

The SUPERBOSS is forever testing his own perceptions against the facts, as others see them.

Performance measurement

For a measure of success you need a measure of performance

In the push for performance too many organisations have gone overboard by drowning their people with innumerable measures. These people seem to spend more time measuring and recording performance than actually performing!

Effective performance requires effective measures, that is, two to four meaningful measures by which your individual contribution can be judged.

The ultimate two measures are, of course, how your customers rate you and bottom-line profitability. These are what the Superboss concentrates on.

A Superboss assesses his own performance and that of his people in terms of these basic measures. That might mean sales results, or improvements to productivity, or maintenance of high levels of quality, or increasing market share with innovative new products, or winning new customers, or completing key projects on time and within budget.

The Superboss does not measure the detailed activities of his people, he measures their results. In other words he measures 'what' they achieve, not 'how' they achieve it. Too many organisations fall into the trap of measuring tasks as opposed to results.

The Superboss never waits for Head Office to impose a measurement system on him and his people. Achieving results is so important to a Superboss that he initiates his own performance measurement process. He agrees with his people the key measures against which their performance will be judged. Customer satisfaction and contribution to profitability will always be key factors in this process.

No matter how objective a Superboss is in measuring performance he accepts that there will always be a subjective element. Ultimately it is customers' perceptions that affect their choices and the success or otherwise of the company.

Before a Superboss measures anyone else he will measure himself. He is his own hardest task-master. He sets himself exceptionally high standards and challenging goals against which he measures himself.

ACTION TODAY

Review your own measures of performance. If they are not already stuck in your mind the probability is that you don't have any effective measures.

What do you think your customers (internal or external) measure you by?

What do you think your shareholders (represented by your senior executives) measure you by?

What do you think your people measure you by?

You must have clear answers to these questions. If you don't, seek advice and find out the answers.

REMEMBER

Everyone measures the performance of a SUPERBOSS.

Politics

There is no profit in management politics

Politics has a bad name and rightly so. When you're out to catch votes you'll say and do anything to be popular, and suppress and hide anything which may have the reverse effect. But people aren't that stupid and tough painful action and blunt words can often win votes. People see through false smiles and become suspicious of those who don't tell them 'the bottom line'.

The Superboss plays no political games, is not out to win the popularity stakes. The Superboss doesn't try to outshine and show up his colleagues, nor drop them in the mire. Nor does he paint a dreadful picture of another department which he then transforms when he takes over.

The Superboss doesn't try to score points or impress the Chairman with his superlative verbal skills. The Superboss doesn't sacrifice other people to cover his own inadequacies, nor does he look for scapegoats when things go wrong. Furthermore he doesn't exaggerate other's inadequacies or his own capabilities.

The Superboss doesn't act behind his boss's back, nor those of his people. The Superboss is not a student of Machiavelli nor does he wish to emulate him.

The Superboss keeps his leadership style honest and straight, speaking his mind in a considered and responsible way. He fights for his company and for his people and is prepared to risk sticking his neck out to do so. His preoccupation is with achieving good results rather than scoring political points.

ACTION TODAY

Make a New Year's resolution (even if it's 23 June) that you will cease to have anything to do with internal politics within the company. You might react in horror, believing that unless you play company politics your survival (let alone promotion) prospects will be greatly reduced. If you're anything like a Superboss, your conscience will be more important than your career. Do you want to work for a company that is going to sacrifice you unless you play its political games?

Concentrate on the task at hand, forget about politics, and think about achieving some excellent results.

REMEMBER

For the SUPERBOSS there's nothing so unproductive as internal politics.

Positiveness

You must be positive to manage people successfully

Never say 'no'! Saying 'no' is the most negative thing a manager can do, and many of them do it frequently.

You might think the corollary is to say 'yes' all the time. Far from it.

In making decisions the Superboss exercises reason and tries to persuade people with it, or conversely they persuade him.

The Superboss is reluctant to reject anything, whether it be an idea, a proposal, a recommendation, a suggestion, or a request for five minutes of his time.

The Superboss will always try to give a positive response, will always try to accept someone's recommendation, will always try to help. He'll disagree with a person from time to time, but the process of disagreement will not be a negative act but one of constructive criticism and help. In avoiding saying 'no' the Superboss will always try to help a person find a way forward.

When you have a team working smoothly and cohesively together, all pointing in the same direction and working hard to achieve a desired goal, any negative decision, statement or act will in effect retard progress by channelling some of the team's energy away from the goal.

In being positive the Superboss will keep that energy harnessed in one direction only. Whilst he might not agree with a request for an additional clerk in Geraldine Shear's section he'll try to help her identify a solution to her specific problem. 'What would you do, Geraldine, if you were in my shoes? Go over budget with an additional clerk, or perhaps see if there's another way of doing the extra work?' The resulting decision will be the most positive for the company and its people.

ACTION TODAY

Take a large box. Stick a label on it and mark it with large letters: 'NO GO AREA'.

Every time you are tempted to make a negative decision look at the box. If you do succumb, make a written note of that negative decision, no matter how trivial, and put it in the box.

At your next team meeting ask your people to estimate how many slips of paper are inside the box. If you are a SUPERBOSS, every team member will bet the right answer every time. That's being positive! Every one a winner!

REMEMBER

The SUPERBOSS is not a permission giver nor a permission refusenik. To be positive the SUPERBOSS is always looking for ways forward to help people achieve their goals.

Praise

Praise the manager who praises his staff

Managers often blame their staff for what is going wrong in their division. It is an unforgivable sin, yet it occurs frequently. Managers complain about 'those girls in the word processing section who are only interested in filling in time between nine and five'. Or 'those villains down in transport will screw the company for everything they can get'. Such managers will even complain about individual members of their own team.

In the Superboss's view, if he can't praise someone in his team, that person shouldn't be a member of it. If he can't praise the team itself, it's because he's hopeless as a team leader.

The Superboss has faith in his people. He knows they give of their best and he'll make a point of praising them for it.

For the Superboss one of life's great satisfactions is to find something good and give praise. For example, he might phone in from outside one day and hear a warm friendly response from the telephone operator who doesn't know it's him.

The next day he'll go and see Bettie Fowler, the switchboard supervisor, and praise her and the team. When he finds that Nikki Powell in Purchasing has secured a 2 per cent price reduction from a main supplier, he'll give high priority to praising her for her contribution.

The praise of a Superboss is never uncritical, always genuine. He doesn't give praise for praise's sake, or use it as a motivational cosmetic to make a person feel good, irrespective of performance. His praise must be earned, for he'll praise only real contribution.

ACTION TODAY

Begin a brand new notebook and print on the cover in large capitals 'PRAISE BOOK'. Take each clean page and write at the top the date for the next 50 consecutive working days (or 100 if the notebook is a fat one).

Your task now is to make an effort each day to praise at least three people, whether it be your immediate reportees or people in their teams. Make a note of who you praise and why. It can be for minor tasks (your secretary has cleaned out the top drawer of your desk) or great achievements (your team exceeded sales quota for the fifth consecutive month). The praise must be genuine and for a real contribution to the company and its people.

REMEMBER

The SUPERBOSS goes out of his way to give praise. For him it is always genuine and spontaneous.

Pride

He who has no pride should have no job.
Take pride in your people, it is your job

Pride is a question of personal honour. There is no honour in not giving of your best at work.

Many people have a thousand reasons for not giving of their best. They feel exploited or underpaid. They feel their working conditions are not good enough, that their company takes them for granted, that they're treated like machines instead of people. They feel that career progression is governed by a political rat race and is unfair. They feel let down by the company, discriminated against. Consequently their pride in what they're doing is diminished. If the company has no pride in them, why should they have pride in what they're doing?

The Superboss is a proud man. He holds his head up high and speaks highly of his people. He tells his family, his neighbours, his friends how great they are. He is proud of what he has done for them; proud of the way he has improved their working conditions; proud of the way they have all been trained; proud of the way so many of them have been promoted out of his department.

Most of all he is proud of what they have done for him, what they have achieved.

His team are proud too. They are proud to work for a Superboss, proud of his reputation, proud of his leadership. They take pride in all aspects of their work: the quality of the product and the service, the housekeeping, the team spirit. They take pride in achieving excellent results and beating the competition.

The Superboss's pride will be hurt sometimes. It will be hurt when his people tell him that the car-parking problem he promised to look into still hasn't been sorted. It will be hurt when he learns his team has slipped three days on a delivery to Blanchard's. It will be hurt when the trusted Jon Andersen is caught thieving. It will be hurt when he forgets to call in and see Ina Ling as promised. But when his pride is hurt he will always take action to redress it.

For the Superboss pride has to be balanced with humility. Too much pride and people become defensive and resistant to suggestions for improvements. Pride can never be an absolute.

ACTION TODAY

You must be proud to be a manager. If you're not proud, stay at home and think very deeply about it.

Be positive. What do you feel proud about at work? What do you feel proud about as a manager? What pride do you take in your people? Do you show pride in them? How? Do you take pride in your results, their results? If you can answer these questions positively, hold your head up high and go to work.

REMEMBER

You can tell a SUPERBOSS by the pride he takes in his people and their results.

Principles

Every manager must have a clear framework of principles within which to manage

You never know where you stand with a manager who lacks a clearly defined set of management principles. It's not that they are dishonest or devious, it's just that they tend to be arbitrary in their decisions, in the views they formulate. Managers who lack principles tend to change their minds frequently, tend to blow with the wind, tend to be nice to you when they want something and ignore you at other times. They are forever in reactive mode.

Managers who lack management principles are managers who don't think. They do what they're told. They say the first thing that comes into their head. They push the paper around, take the telephone calls and are deft at passing on problems to someone else. Such managers are often manipulative, manipulating not only people but words. They avoid commitment by talking their way out of everything, presenting to the uninitiated a glossy façade of management effectiveness and understanding.

For such managers expediency becomes a substitute for principle.

The Superboss is a man of principle. Over the years he has carefully thought through the basic principles of managing people successfully and developed his own personal framework. That framework supports him every minute of his management career. It forms the basis for every decision he makes about people, his behaviour towards them and the initiatives he takes. His principles are those of any superb manager. They are founded on openness, honesty, commitment, co-operation, positiveness, support, people-caring, profit-mindedness and many others. In fact they are the principles which form the framework for this book.

ACTION TODAY

This is an evening job. After dinner (don't drink any wine) diplomatically ask your partner to leave you alone for an hour or two 'to do some thinking'. Turn down the lights and place on your CD player a Mozart piano concerto (or whatever your choice). Shut your eyes and search deep into your heart. Look at your management principles. In all conscience are you completely clear about them? Don't be complacent. Don't con yourself with a quick easy answer. Ask yourself again: 'What are the principles upon which I manage my people on a day-to-day basis?' When you have a genuinely honest answer, ask yourself two difficult questions: 'Do I carry the conviction to apply these principles?' 'Do I sometimes allow expediency to displace my principles?'

Think carefully, think honestly, think twice. Re-establish and re-apply your principles, it's the most important thing you can do.

Then drink a glass of wine with your partner and go to bed.

REMEMBER

Principle is the bed-rock upon which the SUPERBOSS manages.

Priorities

Priorities always come first, so if you want to come first, decide on your priorities

Working out your priorities is a continuous process. The Superboss is doing it all the time.

To achieve his profit objectives, to achieve what he wants for his customers and for his people the Superboss is continually reviewing how to deploy his valuable resources – the time and efforts of his people as well as his own, the money in his budget, the physical equipment at his disposal. The needs of his customers, his company and his people will change day by day and therefore the Superboss's priorities will need to be reviewed day by day.

He might sit down quietly at eight o'clock each morning, before anyone comes into his office, and review his priorities for the day. He might sit down at the weekend, perhaps for half-an-hour before Saturday lunch, and review his priorities for the coming week or month. He might decide to spend less time on training and more on an urgent quality problem or to deploying more resources to retrieve a loss of market share in the North West. He might realise that communications with his team have suffered following the usual mad year end rush and that he needs to assign higher priority to this.

The Superboss will be constantly reviewing priorities with his own boss in the light of ever changing circumstances. He will also review priorities with his team at his regular monthly meeting with them. In the end decisions on priorities will be his, but he will involve those around him as much as possible.

The priorities a Superboss establishes effectively reflect those aspects of his work which he thinks are most important and therefore which he values most. In simple terms this means giving priority to people, customers and profit in that order, for one leads to the other.

ACTION TODAY

List your priorities for (a) today, (b) tomorrow, (c) next week, (d) next month. Try to determine what is most important for the company and your people in the allocation of your time and their time, as well as in the allocation of money.

Having listed your priorities, go and see your boss for an informal chat. Review with him or her (c) and (d) above. Having confirmed these priorities with your boss, discuss them with your team at the next regular meeting.

Don't forget that giving time to your people is a high priority.

REMEMBER

The priorities of a SUPERBOSS are driven by his own personal values.

Problem solving

Most managers are expert at stating problems, few at solving them

A consultant once advised me: 'As soon as you identify a problem you own it'.

But . . .

'I can't motivate my people because the company's pay policy is a real problem.'

'The problem is the company doesn't allow us to manage. We don't even have the authority to send someone on an external seminar.'

'The problem is our finance department, they're so bureaucratic. I get a constant stream of documentation from them. I wish I could press on and do my real job.'

There used to be a little plaque you could buy to put on the wall of your office which said: 'The bad manager finds 48 reasons why a problem cannot be solved. The good manager finds 48 ways of solving that problem'.

If you can't solve a problem, forget it. It's not worth worrying about. If it's going to affect you don't complain, just take some action and do something about it.

The Superboss gets off his backside, finds the heart of the problem and does his best to solve it. If there is a problem with company pay policy, he'll make a case to his boss and to Personnel. It'll be a persuasive case, well researched, well presented and aimed at convincing the decision makers that unless there is a change there will be immense damage to the company. If the problem is supervisory training, the Superboss will demonstrate to his boss the effect the lack of training is having (low efficiency, poor safety record, low morale, high employee turnover, too many customer complaints). He'll convince his boss an investment in training is well worthwhile. He'll also persuade him or her to delegate more authority to him to avoid wasting time on typewriter issues.

If the Superboss sees a problem, he doesn't let it rest. He sets out to solve it, even it if appears that the solution lies in the hands of others. If the problem has an impact on him he'll own it and then he'll convince the others to implement the proposed solution.

ACTION TODAY

This is where, once and for all, you stop the moaning and groaning. Purge your mind of all your management problems. Divide them into two lists:

1 Those you can do something about.
2 Those you can do nothing about.

Destroy the second list and never refer to those problems again. Now set about solving the problems in the first list. You'll be amazed at your ability to persuade people. Don't give up – you will need to persist.

You'll also be amazed at how many problems which originally fell into the second category can be moved to the first.

REMEMBER

If the SUPERBOSS can't solve a problem the first time, he'll try a second and then a third time. He'll keep on trying, a thousand times if necessary, until he solves it.

Promotion

The best managers promote their people rather than themselves

For the Superboss his greatest sacrifice is his greatest pleasure – to promote the very best member of his team to another part of the company.

You must have heard it in those dull dispirited organisations where nobody ever progresses: 'My boss is blocking my promotion' or 'My boss thinks I'm indispensable' or 'My boss is holding me back'. In such companies promotion opportunities are few and far between, and when they do occur the wrong people are perceived to get the job, the right ones are passed over and grieve that they didn't even have a fair chance.

The Superboss will create a dynamic organisation in which promotion opportunities occur frequently. He'll search for them. The last thing he'll do is upgrade all his people's jobs in order to simulate promotion, but he'll do everything possible to create genuine promotion opportunities. He will assign senior people to projects, or other parts of the company so that openings can be created to bring on and promote up-and-coming juniors.

The Superboss will encourage others to compete for promotion. He will encourage them to acquire broad experience, achieve results, develop their skills so that they are in the best position to pursue opportunities. He'll encourage his 'indispensable' finance manager to apply for a transfer to another division, knowing that if this takes place at least three promotion opportunities will occur. (On the subject of promotion nobody is 'indispensable' to the Superboss.)

The Superboss will make certain that all suitable candidates are given a fair and equal opportunity to obtain a career advance. Promotion decisions will be arrived at in a rigorously objective manner after painstaking consideration of each candidate.

ACTION TODAY

If nobody's been promoted from your area within the last year, you're a failure, and so is the company. Start now and create some genuine promotion opportunities. Recognise that for each person promoted nine others will be disappointed. Even so the prospects will encourage competition and development.

If you can't identify a promotion opportunity for one of your people within the next three months, either resign or ask for a transfer. That will create one.

REMEMBER

For the SUPERBOSS promoting his people is the hallmark of success.

Push for excellence

If a manager doesn't push for excellence, what does he or she push for?

Some managers don't push. In fact they allow others to push them around – their bosses, their colleagues, their people. A manager might even have a reputation for being a 'pushover,' for giving people whatever they want.

The Superboss doesn't sit back and wait to be pushed. He's out there in front pushing for excellence, for higher standards of performance, for an even bigger contribution by his team to the company's profit.

The Superboss is able to push hard because he's very clear about what he has to achieve and very confident about the capabilities of his people. He'll push them for additional sales revenue, for additional production output, for excellent customer service, for excellent quality, for excellent housekeeping. He'll push them for an excellent safety record and for excellent employee relations, accepting only a positive cohesive co-operative style of team work.

The Superboss pushes for excellence, recognises it and rewards it with praise, giving constructive feedback to those who are not quite there. To achieve excellence the Superboss selects only the very best people and ensures they receive the very best training and development. When his team are round the table he'll make sure they are very clear about the standards of excellence he wants them to achieve. He defines excellence in terms of best practice for every aspect of the team's operation.

The Superboss pushes for excellence because he knows that every person in his area wants to be proud of an excellent performance and furthermore wants the support of a Superboss to achieve it.

ACTION TODAY

Complete on one sheet of paper an 'Excellence Analysis'. Draw two columns. On the left list all the areas where your team and their people have demonstrated their excellence through best practice. Don't be afraid to put down items of individual excellence.

In the right-hand column list 'Opportunity Areas' where you feel your team are not quite achieving excellence. (There must be some opportunity, they can't be that excellent!) On this occasion do not list individual opportunity areas (take those up separately).

If you have no idea of what constitutes excellence through best practice in your area, you're already an abysmal failure.

ACTION NEXT WEEK

Convene your team and discuss with them your 'Excellence Analysis'. Modify it as appropriate. Then go out, you and your team, and push for excellence by developing best practice all round.

REMEMBER

The SUPERBOSS doesn't expect perfection, but he does expect excellence through consistent best practice.

Question

There are no easy answers in management, only difficult questions

If you know all the answers you probably haven't asked the right questions. In this competitive world there are no easy answers as to how to make profit, how to achieve really effective employee relations. The scene changes daily; new factors arise, organisations change, people move on, sales drop, unexpected orders come in, new competition appears and so on. Even on the shopfloor, where a routine production operation exists, things are changing all the time; absenteeism goes up, the standard of housekeeping goes down, suddenly a fault will occur on a packing machine you haven't had a problem with for five years.

The Superboss is alert to all these events, has an inquisitive mind, is always asking questions. 'Why this?' 'Why that?' Not that he doesn't trust his people, not that he wants to interfere. He just wants to know what's going on. By asking the right question at the right time he might come up with the answer that has eluded everyone else, might find a way through when nobody else could.

In fact the Superboss has a talent, some would say instinct, for arriving at the root of the problem in second to no time. The Superboss has that canny ability to listen carefully when a serious problem arises, ask one or two apparently innocuous questions and then intuitively point towards the solution.

The Superboss spends much of his time diplomatically questioning people. 'Why didn't we use the ten-ton truck for that trip?' 'Why didn't Tubby Wagg show up for work yesterday?' 'Why have we shut down that cooling chamber three times in the last week?' 'Why aren't you smiling today, Sandra?'

The Superboss is always questioning his team, challenging them, keeping them on their mettle. Not because he doesn't trust them, but because he knows that without questioning people tend to become slovenly in their judgements, narrow in their outlook. No one person can see everything. The Superboss, with his well directed questions, helps his people and himself to see more.

ACTION TODAY

Take your normal walk around and discipline yourself to question any single thing you do not understand. Why is that container lying unused in the corner? Why are those men sitting talking nervously in the canteen? Why haven't we had a reply from Calan's?

You will expect the people responsible to know the answers. If they don't, then perhaps you can help them. If you know the answers, don't ask the questions.

REMEMBER

The SUPERBOSS knows that to answer to his own boss he first has to ask the right questions.

Recognition

Every individual needs recognition

The most neglected area of management is recognition. Frequently people complain that their hard work goes unnoticed by managers, that their own individual contributions are not appreciated, not valued.

Too many managers find it all too easy to criticise when jobs go wrong but then fail miserably to recognise the substantial efforts people make on 99 per cent of occasions. No wonder people become demoralised and say 'Is it really worth the effort?'

It is easy to take people's hard work for granted, to assume it is the norm and do nothing about it.

One of the human being's most basic needs is to feel valued and appreciated by the people around. People need the reinforcement that recognition brings – it enhances their self-esteem and feelings of personal worth. Most people are sincere in their efforts to do their best for the company, to make as valuable a contribution as they can.

The Superboss recognises this and goes out of his way to communicate his recognition and appreciation of individual effort. There is no one simple technique for this. Like the 'one minute manager' he tries to find people doing something right. He loves to identify success and achievement. He loves to see people working hard. He loves to see people cracking seemingly intractable problems. All this gives him cause to demonstrate his recognition of their endeavours. It might be a shake of the hand, or a thumbs up sign, or a little note expressing thanks, or a small gift, or a meal out one Friday evening.

In expressing recognition the Superboss is spontaneous and avoids routine. He would never want his people to expect recognition as of a right.

The Superboss also encourages other people to demonstrate their recognition of the efforts of his team. For example he'll invite the Chief Executive to come and say a few words at the next team meeting. Or he'll ask a journalist from the local newspaper to write up one of the team's main achievements.

Recognition creates pride and the momentum to continue the good work.

ACTION TODAY

Record here the action you have taken over the last month to recognise the considerable efforts of your team.

Itemise each one of these efforts and then produce a further plan of action to demonstrate your appreciation.

REMEMBER

People always recognise a SUPERBOSS.

Reliability

Product reliability, profit reliability and service reliability reflect the reliability of management

Reliability, or lack of it, is a reflection of an organisation's culture, of its infrastructure and of the influence its managers have within it.

If you can rely on the Chief Executive to achieve a result, more likely than not you can rely on every person in the organisation to do the same. If you can rely on the Vice-President of Marketing to keep his or her word, more likely than not you can rely on every person in Marketing to do the same.

Reliability is a value upon which the Superboss places great store. He prides himself on his own reliability as well as insisting that his people are reliable too. If the Superboss makes a promise to a customer, you can rely on him keeping it. For example, when the Superboss visits an off-base location and informally says he'll look into a problem raised, then you can rely on him looking into that problem and reporting back.

The Superboss stresses to his team the importance of reliability. 'I don't want the employee representatives coming in here telling me you haven't installed the drinking fountains you promised for three months ago.' He stresses the importance of reliability as far as the customer is concerned. 'If you told Hillard's you'd deliver Friday, then I'm afraid you have got no option. You deliver Friday or take the consequences of your lack of reliability'.

The Superboss knows that reliability runs alongside accountability as a key element in the successful management of people. The reliability of a Superboss helps establish his credibility and reputation. It helps establish trust and respect. Most importantly, it is the cornerstone of the company's future success, because the risks are minimised when you have a reliable Superboss.

ACTION TODAY

Undertake a 'Reliability Analysis'. Write down all recent commitments by yourself and your people. Tick off those where the commitment has been honoured. Call up your team and give urgent attention to the balance. Areas of unreliability should be of a serious concern.

ACTION TOMORROW

Analyse any complaints you have received, either internally or externally, for lack of reliability in your department over the last twelve months. Prepare a bar chart with one red bar unit for each complaint. Keep a twelve-months running total and plot your progress in improving reliability month by month.

REMEMBER

The SUPERBOSS never compromises reliability by accepting or making excuses.

Reporting relationships

Everyone should know who their immediate boss is – without that there can be no authority nor reporting relationship

It might sound obvious that you should know who your immediate boss is, but there are some companies where this is not the case.

In one company a group of over 300 people named the same person as their boss. The operations staff, the customer-liaison people, the supervisors and a few others all named the Operations Manager as their boss.

The hard-working supervisors worked different shifts from the operations staff and tended to act as progress chasers and problem solvers for each period of duty. With employees seeing a different supervisor each shift a dangerous supervisory vacuum arose. These people effectively had no permanent boss and this led, over a period time, to a virtually uncontrollable employee relations situation.

The Superboss places high priority in establishing formal and clear reporting lines throughout his organisation, whether it number 10 people or 10,000. He expects to know his own boss and he expects every person in his organisation to know theirs. The Superboss appreciates that matrix reporting lines are sometimes inevitable, for example where the divisional accountant might report directly to the divisional director and additionally report professionally to the group finance director.

The Superboss will spend a considerable amount of time working at these reporting lines and ensuring that accountabilities are very clear. He knows that for people to perform effectively they must have an immediate boss who sees them regularly, who can recognise their individual contribution, who can give them feedback on how to improve their skills, who can help them address their individual problems, who can encourage them to do better and finally who can hold them accountable. Also every employee needs an immediate boss to turn to for advice, for decisions and for help.

ACTION TODAY

Examine the organisation chart for your section, department, division or company. (If there isn't an up-to-date one, shame on you. Draw it up immediately.) Cast an eagle eye over it for 'funny' reporting lines, lines that go round corners, duck under others or bypass levels of command. Question any such irregularities. Are they necessary? Unless you have a very clean organisation with clear reporting lines for everyone (which will be the case in good companies with Superbosses) start thinking how you might clear up the mess. Forget about people and make sure that each job has a clear-cut reporting line to a higher level job. To help with this clarification process call in your local organisation expert, whether he or she be an external consultant, someone from Personnel or a key member of your team. Spend some days carefully thinking through how you're going to clear up these relationships.

Then consider carefully how you will implement any changes.

Don't push this page aside and take it for granted your reporting relationships are clear. The disease is more widespread than most people think.

REMEMBER

You must clarify your reporting relationships to be a SUPERBOSS.

Resilience

When everyone else has given up, the resilient manager will still be there, and will succeed

It's one of those days! The phone never stops ringing, there's a queue of people at your door with urgent problems, the mail is piling up, you have to be at the sales office two miles down the road within ten minutes, and now, to make matters worse your boss has called you in on some urgent matter.

This is when the Superboss will relax a little, sip some water and do some thinking.

He won't panic, he'll just call in his secretary and calmly give her some instructions. 'Ring the sales office please and apologise to them that I'll be along five minutes late. I'm going to leave the mail till this evening unless there's any dynamite there. Now who is it outside? I'll have five seconds with Rebecca Weill and sign that urgent travel authorisation, but perhaps you'll ask Mick Clarke and Sylvia Donne to come back after lunch. Meanwhile I'd better make that quick phone call to Paul Gates.'

The Superboss is resilient. He can take the pressure. He takes it as it comes, constantly reordering his priorities but never letting others down. He is imperturbable, knowing that he is doing his best. You will never see a Superboss panic, never hear him cry out in despair. You will never hear him yell at people when the pressure's on.

When the pressure is on, the Superboss will take everything in his stride, calmly tackling the priority problems but taking care not to neglect the everyday needs of his people. When the pressure's on, the Superboss doesn't try to do everything himself, he delegates, sometimes waits. When the pressure's on, the Superboss is in control, not out of control, that's how resilient he is.

ACTION TODAY

Find an old Christmas or birthday card. Turn it inside out and write on the blank side: RESILIENCE. WHEN THE PRESSURE'S ON, TAKE TWO MINUTES OFF AND THINK.

Leave that card on your desk so that nobody else can see it. Study it for two minutes next time you feel you're under pressure.

Then address the problem. You'll be surprised how a little thinking time in mid-crisis can help make you resilient.

REMEMBER

The SUPERBOSS is so resilient you will never see him tearing his hair out or even torn apart.

Respect

Without mutual respect it is impossible to motivate and manage people effectively

The demonstration of disrespect is one of the most worrying features of many organisations. Management have no respect for many of their people. Many people have no respect for their people and show it with wile in many ways. Sales departments have no respect for personnel, and personnel have no respect for operations. Archie Tolworth, supervisor, has no respect for his, in his view, incompetent boss Dave Smith, and in turn Dave Smith, the Production Manager, has no respect for Clive Manning, the new Operations Director the company has just brought in.

The culture of disrespect, instead of producing profit, produces much finger pointing and backbiting and in the end a loss of confidence in the company, its products, its management and its people. Disrespect undermines the effectiveness of the organisation.

You'll recognise a Superboss. Talk to his people. They respect him. Talk to him. He respects his people. He respects the fact that each person has a vital contribution to make towards the success of the company. He also respects that each person is an individual with individual needs, problems and inadequacies. He respects that each individual needs help as much as he does.

The Superboss shows respect in the courteous and polite way he treats people and talks to them. He respects that whoever they are they have a viewpoint. He therefore always listens carefully.

The Superboss respects a person for all his or her good points and tries to help him or her overcome the bad points. He respects the trade unions, not because he necessarily agrees with them all the time – he doesn't – but because they are there because his people want them there, and they have an important role to play.

With mutual respect the Superboss treats everyone in the way that he would want to be treated. If a person shows disrespect, he'll confront the issue with respect. Then he'll forgive and forget.

ACTION TODAY

Be honest! Cast your mind back to your last gossip session (perhaps yesterday at lunch with one or two of your colleagues). Try to remember who you criticised behind their backs. Perhaps you said to your closest colleague: 'I don't know what that crazy Chief Executive is doing, cutting back on travel. He's an idiot! How can I do my job?'

Try to identify the 'plus' points of whoever you criticised (behind their backs). There will be many. Discipline yourself to concentrate on these 'plus' points next time you speak about that person. Show some respect.

REMEMBER

For whatever you're worth, the SUPERBOSS will respect you.

Responsibility

Responsibility is that difficult-to-define burden carried on a manager's back

There is a distinct difference between responsibility, authority and accountability. Authority is the power vested in a manager to make specific decisions (for example, on expenditure or recruitment) or to speak on behalf of the company.

Accountability is the requirement for managers to account for the decisions they make and for the successes or failures these decisions lead to.

Responsibility is much broader. To be responsible is to carry a personal burden for everything you control in your area and to bear the consequence of the actions under your control. The consequence of that action might have an impact on other employees, customers and the community. Responsibility embraces authority and accountability. Responsibility is the total burden and in any management job it is very difficult to define.

If a manager treats an employee harshly and aggressively, and soon after that employee suffers a breakdown, is the manager responsible?

If a manager tries to save money by contracting with a cheaper but less well-known supplier, and then that supplier goes bust, is the manager responsible for non-delivery?

The mark of a Superboss is that he'll carry responsibility for everything that happens within his area. He won't shrug off responsibility and blame suppliers or an individual's lack of mental fitness. The Superboss feels responsible if his decisions have repercussions in his people's private lives. He feels responsible if he inadvertently lets down his customers, or if he fails to take good advice from one of his people.

For the Superboss responsibility is a matter of conscience. If mistakes are made in his area, and they often are, he won't attempt to assign blame for the failure to his boss, nor to the company's poor policies, nor to his people for not understanding. The Superboss will accept the responsibility.

ACTION TODAY

Answer these questions:

Do you feel responsible for your people?
Do you feel responsible for their selection?
Do you feel responsible for their training?
Do you feel responsible for their welfare?
Do you feel responsible for their morale?
Do you feel responsible for the impact of your decisions on their private lives?
Do you feel responsible for their careers?
Do you feel responsible for their pay?
Do you feel responsible for their performance?
Do you feel responsible for what they achieve?
AGAIN: Do you feel responsible for your people?

Should any answer be 'No', think very carefully and ask the question again. If you're not responsible for the performance of your people, who is? If you're not responsible for the other factors contributing to performance, who is?

Should each answer be 'Yes', think very carefully. Do you really mean it? Do you? Do you feel responsible for your people?

REMEMBER

First and foremost the SUPERBOSS is responsible for his own actions.

Results

Results are the only measure of a manager's performance

Some managers don't pass stage one. Stage one differentiates between the task and the end result. To use a simple example, a bus driver's job is not merely to drive a bus (that's just a task), but to deliver passengers safely and on time from Point A to Point B (the result).

Some managers think that their job is to carry out the task of pushing paper around (for example, signing expenses), to attend committee meetings and mouth comments, to go and have a chat with the gang, or to drink tea with employee representatives. Such managers think that the method of their job (the actual process of doing it) is the job.

The Superboss sees things differently. He sees his job as achieving a distinct business result for the company. In line management jobs, that result might be achieving a sales quota or a production target. In a staff management job, it might be achieving a certain volume of cost-effective training or a target number of new recruits by a given date.

The results a Superboss achieves relate to his objectives. Provided the law is not broken, company policies and procedures not breached, human dignity not impaired, the Superboss is far less interested in the methods his staff use than in the results they achieve. Although the Superboss might help them develop their methods, he won't 'police' them. You won't see, for example, a Superboss looking out of the window at 8.30 am each morning counting how many people are arriving late. He won't issue memos telling people to tighten up on punctuality or to use both sides of a sheet of paper.

The Superboss is results-oriented rather than method-mad. He knows that the means to an end are not an end in themselves. It's easy to kick a football, much more difficult to score a goal.

ACTION TODAY

Concentrate your attention on the results you have to achieve during the next month. Write them down, become preoccupied with their achievement. Each result must be measurable, either qualitatively or quantitatively. Whilst you might examine your own methods of achieving these results, leave your staff to determine their methods. Help them where possible. Avoid imposing methods. ('You must do it this way' is bad. 'You must achieve this' is better.)

REMEMBER

You only become a SUPERBOSS as a result of what you achieve.

Reviews

Always review progress first and people second

Profit through people. People come first. You cannot profit without them.

But when considering the review process, you should look at the results first, and only then at the person who's achieved those results.

If you attempt to review the person first you'll soon lose sight of the results. You'll be reviewing Abdullah Raoul's behaviour. (Is being aggressive a good or bad quality?) You'll be reviewing Jan Francis's ability to communicate. (Is talking too little a good or bad habit?) You'll be reviewing the number of hours put in by Alphonse Hoddard. (Does working long hours lead to better results?) You'll be reviewing the person, but not the results.

The Superboss undertakes periodic progress reviews. He'll bring his team round the table every Monday morning and spend half an hour reviewing what results were achieved last week. Perhaps once a month he might devote half a day for an in-depth review of progress year-to-date against budget.

In addition to team reviews the Superboss carries out a periodic review with each member of his team, perhaps once a month. He'll review the results Abdullah Raoul achieved on the sales front and see once again that his successes are sporadic. He'll trace this to his temperamental behaviour. Having reviewed the results the Superboss will then, if necessary, review the person. Sometimes it's not necessary. Despite Jan Francis's personal problems and her shy retiring manner, she consistently shows she can get the business. He only needs to look at Jan's results. However, there's a problem with Alphonse Hoddard. Alphonse always arrives at the office before him and is always there after he leaves. In spite of this he can't seem to produce the accounts on time. The results are unsatisfactory, so the Superboss will review what he can do to help.

ACTION TODAY

You can't know what progress you are making unless you systematically review it. Check your diary and make sure that you have regular progress review meetings with your team, and separately with each individual. Discipline yourself to look only at the results to begin with and then, if need be, at the person.

In reviewing the results relate them to the objectives you agreed earlier and for which each person is accountable.

REMEMBER

In reviewing progress a SUPERBOSS is measuring your contribution to the company's success.

Rewards

The worst form of reward is money

Pavlov's theory went out of fashion a long time ago. You cannot treat people like dogs. They're more intelligent and will quickly learn how to beat the system by obtaining the reward without giving the desired response.

In the management vocabulary, rewards should be differentiated from incentives. A reward is a form of recognition after the event, whilst an incentive is an enticement before the event.

Recognition of an employee's contribution is necessary and it is important from time to time to reward an exceptional contribution. Although there is nothing intrinsically wrong with giving monetary rewards, it has the danger of corrupting the pay system and demotivating the very people you want to motivate.

The Superboss maintains a great reservoir of rewards, mostly non-financial. It starts with a smile or a pat on the back. It goes on to be a letter of appreciation or a telephone call and could end up by being a dinner on the company, a bunch of flowers or a bottle of whisky. Once a year when something exceptional has happened he might authorise a short overseas company-paid vacation for someone. It will have to be exceptional and the Superboss will be highly discriminating in making the decision. He'll be confident about the precedent and that there will be no pressure to breach it. (If an employee's invention to recycle scrap saved the company half a million, would you begrudge as a reward a short overseas trip paid for by the company?)

When people work for the Superboss they don't aim to receive rewards. The satisfaction of achieving good results is sufficient. They trust their Superboss enough to know that when they put themselves out with some exceptional performance he will reward them. And he will. He'll call them in at the end of a long hard day, pass round the beer and wine and reward them with a smile and a brief word of thanks.

ACTION TODAY

Initiate your own rewards ceremony. For example, if you run an office convene the ceremony for 4.00 pm on the last Friday of next month. Consult your team and brainstorm as many types of rewards as possible. (For example, a reward for the friendliest person on the third floor, for the person who typed the most memos, for the person who stayed on late to take an urgent overseas phone call.) The rewards should be of minimal value (a bar of chocolate, a pen, a bottle of aspirins). You should serve tea, coffee and biscuits. Make it an enjoyable occasion and then announce that in six months time you'll be giving a reward to the person who devises the most original list of rewards.

If you lead a team of hardworking office staff, take them out for a Chinese meal next Saturday night and at the end of the dinner make a little speech and reward each one of them with a pair of chopsticks.

REMEMBER

The SUPERBOSS seeks no reward other than the satisfaction of seeing his people do well.

Rules

Rules should be common sense. As a rule, a manager should not be a ruler

Rules exist for the general welfare of every person in the company.

Good companies always have a little booklet listing the rules. 'No alcohol on the premises. White hats and coats must be worn in all food preparation areas', and so on.

The Superboss knows when he can break the rules. Only because it's common sense. 'Look, Anita', he'll say to his new secretary on her first day, 'the rule of this company is that you start at 9 am, have forty minutes for lunch between 12 noon and 2 pm and finish at 5.30 pm. Now it's no problem if you want to arrive a little late one day, say 9.30 am, work through your lunch hour or stay a little late. We're prepared to be flexible in this department.'

The Superboss will fight for an exception to the rules when he feels it appropriate. He'll go to the travel department and say to the supervisor: 'Margo, I know the rules with regard to air travel for supervisory staff, but Arnold Hamilton has volunteered to fly to New York on Friday, work all through Saturday and most of Sunday to fix that urgent customer problem and then return Sunday night for that vital engineering review meeting on Monday afternoon. He's sacrificing his whole weekend and I want a business-class ticket for him. If you won't accept my authority for breaking the rules, then you and I have a problem. Let's go upstairs to Dick Tauber's office and resolve it there.'

But when the Superboss is not occasionally breaking the rules he's ensuring for the rest of the time that people are keeping them. He won't turn a blind eye if Andy Calver isn't wearing safety shoes, or if Dickie Bird parks in the visitors' car park when it's raining. Rules are there to be respected and the Superboss makes sure they are. Every time they are broken without his authority it undermines that authority and reduces his credibility in the eyes of others.

ACTION TODAY

This is an easy one. Examine your company rules booklet and remind yourself what's in it. Don't go looking for anyone breaking the rules (that's a witch hunt, and is unnecessary). Keep the rules at the back of your mind and take action should you come across an abuse.

If there are no company rules, take the initiative and write them. Send them to Employee Relations, ask them to consult the appropriate people and then issue them.

REMEMBER

For the SUPERBOSS the fewer the rules the better.

Security

Security of employment should be second only to security of profits as a strategic management objective

There is an argument that if you make people too secure in their jobs they'll become complacent, inefficient, take everything for granted and will not give of their all. But it's an irrelevant argument.

In today's world no employee can be fully secure, because in a competitive environment profit can never be fully secure. A simple fact of life which often escapes people is that an organisation needs revenue, not only to finance wages but also to make profit and give a return to those who have risked their own money to invest in the company. Never forget the shareholders.

The Superboss reminds his people of this when from time to time they become lulled into the illusion that the company is a bottomless reservoir of money. 'The best way you can keep your jobs and salaries secure', he will tell them 'is to give of your best'.

No company, and therefore no Superboss, can guarantee security of employment. Even so the Superboss will see any attack on his people's jobs as a last resort and to that extent he'll fight to protect them. For example, if there has to be a choice between cutting marketing costs or jobs, he'll cut marketing costs, even if he has to slash his huge but precious advertising budget. He wants his staff to be secure in the knowledge that pay and jobs, in that order, will always be the last to be cut.

The Superboss also attempts to provide security on a day-by-day basis. He doesn't want others to feel insecure because they don't know what's going on, or don't know what he's thinking of them. He doesn't want them to be suspicious about arbitrary decisions being made behind their backs. The Superboss therefore believes that straight talking and honest communication will minimise any feelings of insecurity employees might have. He knows that people work best when they feel secure; that if they feel insecure they will worry, fret, and waste time huddling in corners chatting. The Superboss therefore attempts to make their jobs and pay secure, but without being able to guarantee it.

ACTION TODAY

Do you know how secure your people feel with respect to you and the company? First, ask how secure you feel yourself? Should you feel insecure, then address that issue today. Discuss it with your boss, ascertain the facts and work hard to minimise the insecurity, for yourself and for your people.

But never offer guarantees.

REMEMBER

A SUPERBOSS and his team are only as secure as the profitable performance of the company allows and their expertise provides.

Selection

When you select the person, you select a potential contribution to profit

Selection starts here. The process is vital to the future success of any company.

You would have thought that was glaringly obvious, but there are many companies where managers fail to give sufficient time to this critical task (ask any recruitment specialist).

Such managers will change interview dates four times in four weeks, or cram a fifteen-minute interview between two other meetings and then spend the whole interview talking themselves. They'll refuse to give any time to the important task of discussing with Recruitment the main requirements for the job and the ideal candidate they're looking for. They'll finally select someone with blue eyes.

The Superboss gives the highest priority to selecting the best person for the job. He'll spend a considerable amount of time on it and involve many other additional opinions. Where appropriate he'll use selection techniques such as psychometric testing and assessment centres. At the interview he'll allow the candidate to do most of the talking (although he will need to persuade the candidate that it's a company worth joining, and that he's a Superboss to work for). The Superboss will invite other people to interview the shortlist candidates and he'll value their judgement, especially if someone raises doubts about his preferred choice.

Although the Superboss will do his best to ensure that the selected candidate meets the required specification, he'll occasionally take a risk. He'll use his intuition and, on the basis of the candidate's personality, attitude and potential, select someone who doesn't have all the required experience. In the case of selection, skill and potential are often more important than experience.

The Superboss never allows subjective considerations or prejudice to influence his selection decisions. He works within the law, does not countenance discrimination, and will objectively select the best person.

ACTION TODAY

Ask your recruitment specialist to set up a formal review meeting on selection methods in your department. The objective will be to improve them. It is vital that you always select the best person for the job, and that requires time.

At the review critically examine how much time you invest in the selection of any one individual. Unless you're a Superboss you'll probably find it's insufficient and you are making rushed choices. (The average selection will take about ten hours of the Superboss's time.)

REMEMBER

By selecting the right people in the first place you are on the route to becoming a SUPERBOSS.

Sounding board

A sounding board is an instrument for turning organisation noise into harmonic progress

We all need someone to talk with informally and confidentially; someone off whom we can bounce ideas, with whom we can let off steam, to whom we can moan and groan. No person can be an island.

Managers are no different. They need someone at work to turn to in total confidence for a second opinion, to test out crazy ideas or with whom to relax for three to thirty minutes.

The Superboss has one or two close colleagues whom he uses as a sounding board. He might call in to see them for a quick coffee early in the morning, or just before going home. He'll have a chat, ask for their opinions on things going on.

But the Superboss has other sounding boards too. He will be constantly sounding out people in his area about important issues. At the end of his weekly team briefing he might say: 'Just before we close, I'd welcome your views about this new job evaluation system that employee relations are proposing'.

When he walks round and talks to the cleaners at night, he'll sound them out on what they think of the proposed new layout. The Superboss will also use his own boss as a sounding board, taking him into his confidence about important changes he is planning.

He also encourages other people to use him as a sounding board – his junior staff to sound out new ideas on him, or his immediate subordinates to sound him out on solving problems. The Superboss will always lend a sympathetic, understanding ear.

ACTION TODAY

Set up a series of monthly one-hour 'sounding board sessions'. Anyone in your area can attend (first come, first served, maximum 20). At each meeting everyone is free to raise issues, ideas, problems, which they want to sound out in the group and also with the boss.

As you've initiated the session perhaps you should start the ball rolling by sounding out the group on a couple of ideas you have. Leave plenty of time for them to sound you out on other issues.

REMEMBER

If you have a SUPERBOSS, you will already be on his sounding board.

Standards

Every manager needs standards

Nobody would deny that you cannot manage without standards. The problem is that in many companies standards are not very well defined and, what is worse, not applied. Just look at the difference in service between a good restaurant and a poor one. The difference is one of management standards. The same applies to airlines. Most seasoned travellers can tell you a hundred 'war stories' about varying standards in airlines.

It's not only service standards, but also standards of report writing, of presentation, of dress, of behaviour and many others.

The Superboss sees the definition and maintenance of standards as a key management task. The standards he sets are crystal clear, are understood by everyone in his division and, equally importantly, accepted as being necessary. Let's take, for example, standards of dress. These days the Superboss will recognise that people require a high degree of freedom in deciding how to dress. He will therefore develop a standard which gives scope for this (though he would not allow dress which outrages customers, the visitors or the immediate team). Cliff French's green hair might just be acceptable, whilst Val Sanders' cool bra-less attire with a see-through blouse might not!

The Superboss will also set standards for the recruitment people relating to the efficiency of their response to unsolicited applications. He'll set standards of housekeeping in the canteen. He'll set standards of appearance for company vehicles. He'll set standards for supervisory training, for performance appraisal and for written communications.

Having set the standards, having made sure that they are understood and accepted, he'll establish controls to maintain them. Nothing reduces the credibility of a manager more than when he or she sets a standard and then doesn't attempt to maintain it.

ACTION TODAY

Arrange for an item 'Standards' to be put on the agenda of your next team meeting. At that meeting review with your team what they consider to be the main standards of performance and behaviour in your division. Before the meeting do some careful preparation so that you, as leader of the team, can spell out what you consider to be the most important standards. Make sure that your team agree on the control procedures and that these are followed.

ACTION NEXT WEEK

At your team meeting review whether or not these standards have been achieved.

REMEMBER

The SUPERBOSS sets the highest possible standards and maintains them.

Stress

Stress is good for you – if you think otherwise it will be bad for you

Stress has had a bad press recently, mainly because it is making people ill. Daily we read articles on the increasing stress of everyday life (at work and at home) and on stress-related illnesses virtually becoming an epidemic.

The Superboss loves stress. In fact the only time he is stressed is when he has no stress. Then he is bored and irritable.

The human body is hugely resilient and has an in-built adrenalin system to help it cope with the highest levels of stress. The key however is to cope with stress. It's when you can't cope that you suffer. It's not the stress that causes the problems but the lack of coping.

The Superboss has a simple way of coping with stress. He evaluates the pressure, or the demand, or the problem and decides whether or not he can do something about it. If he can do nothing then he won't worry, because there's nothing he can do about it. If he can do something about it, he'll do it.

In other words there are only two options for dealing with a stressful situation: (a) do something and solve the problem, (b) do nothing because nothing can be done. To cope with stress you have to evaluate which is the appropriate option. If it's the latter, and nothing can be done, then you simply have to tolerate and accept the situation. After all we do not and never will live in a perfect world and therefore we have to learn to live with problems we can do nothing about.

Stress is often caused by uncertainty, especially of other people's behaviour and the potential negative impact this might have on us. The Superboss copes with uncertainty by maximising the certainty of his own mind and his own approach. He minimises the potential damage that can be inflicted on him as a result of the uncertainty of other people's behaviour or other situations. He minimises his dependency on others for motivation and emotional sustenance and increasingly becomes self-reliant in driving himself forward.

Stress-related illnesses result from the fear of being unable to cope. That is a fear of yourself, not of others. By addressing and eliminating his own fears the Superboss copes with stress.

ACTION TODAY

Identify those situations which stress you most and try to analyse the cause. Is it uncertainty, fear of the unknown or fear of your inability to cope that is the cause?

Think carefully through your options for dealing with these stressful situations and determine whether or not you can do anything about each one. If the answer is that you can do nothing, then stop worrying and press on with those circumstances you can do something about.

To eliminate your fears about things you cannot cope with you must learn to accept that you cannot do anything about them. You must also learn to deploy your energies only into problems you can cope with and help to resolve.

REMEMBER

Stress is a positive force in the life of a SUPERBOSS.

Style

To achieve distinction in management you need style

Style is a mark of distinction. Style differentiates one company's approach to management from another. It differentiates the good manager from the bad. Style is the distinctive way in which a manager behaves, in which he or she appears, in which he or she expresses him or herself.

Excellent companies set out to develop a distinguished style of management, one which they know will optimise their chances of success and with which excellent managers will readily identify.

The Superboss favours a style of management which is open and honest, is both results- and people-oriented, is communicative, co-operative and decisive. It is a hard-working, positive and constructive style of management with an equal concern for the company and its people.

The Superboss has developed his style over a number of years. He still thinks carefully about it and always tries to behave consistently. Furthermore, although allowing his supervisors and managers to develop their own personal styles, he encourages them to align it as far as possible with that of the company and himself. If the Superboss has a warm outgoing style, then he won't insist that a quiet and slightly reserved supervisor changes to the same. However, he will encourage that supervisor to develop a style based on trust and mutual respect, on sincerity and integrity, a style compatible with that of the Superboss and his team.

Whilst the Superboss does not want each of his team to be personality clones of himself, he does want them to develop a distinctive, professional and positive style which they can all identify with and feel confident in.

Absence of identifiable style leads to concern about unpredictable behaviour and arbitrariness. People want their leader to have a well-defined style because they will then know where they stand with him.

ACTION TODAY

Call in a consultant or your closest confidant at work and ask him or her to describe honestly your style of management. Does the description accord with your own view? Discuss it, evaluate it and then look for opportunities of improving your style. Perhaps you come across as a waffler, a ditherer, a procrastinator; or as being indecisive, always passing the buck. Ask yourself why another manager along the road appears to be positively the opposite. Perhaps you can learn by observing that manager's style and those of other successful managers.

REMEMBER

You can distinguish a SUPERBOSS by his style.

Support

When the company supports its employees, its employees will support the company

Do you see people as costs or assets?

Costs must be attacked, reduced and minimised. Costs are a necessary evil that detract from profit. Costs are what blunt axes are wielded against when there's a downturn in profit. Costs are not to be supported.

Assets are the items you invest in and the substance from which profit is derived. Assets have to be protected, maintained and developed. They are at the heart of the business. Assets must be supported.

The Superboss sees his people as assets in the organisation. Their support for the company is an asset. He knows that he cannot achieve their support unless he supports them with good pay, good training, good working conditions, good tools, good back-up services and good leadership. They will be aware of his genuine support.

However, his support is not only physical in terms of pay and working conditions, he gives them moral support too. He has their interests at heart and will support them in the pursuit of these interests (albeit not at the expense of the company, they are the company). He'll support them in fixing problems, he'll support them in any profit-making improvements. His support shows and they appreciate it and reciprocate.

The Superboss will also support every individual in his area (whether he or she be one of 10, 100 or 1,000). He'll support and protect that individual's rights as an employee. He'll support any fair cause that has to be fought on behalf of that employee. He'll give moral support when problems arise, when help is needed. He'll lend support with encouragement, warmth and advice whenever it's required.

ACTION TODAY

Find an opportunity of offering support to at least three people today.

Forget about yourself completely and put yourself in the shoes of whoever you meet. Discuss problem areas, opportunity areas and see if you can identify a way of supporting them to solve their problems, exploiting their opportunities.

Set yourself the objective of developing a reputation as a supportive manager.

REMEMBER

The SUPERBOSS supports his people all the time, not only when he wants something.

Systems

There is no system that can be substituted for managing people successfully

You might have thought that personnel systems were taking over the process of managing people. All you had to do was fill in the forms: the appraisal documents, the performance indicator sheets, the climate surveys, the assessment centre tests, the psychometric tests, the succession plans, the training needs analyses, career review forms, the briefing sheets and, finally, the termination reports.

Well here's a breath of fresh air. The Superboss doesn't have any of that nonsense. To be more accurate, he doesn't subscribe to all the latest pseudo-scientific techniques peddled by the gurus from across the Atlantic.

But don't delude yourself. The Superboss knows that underpinning some of these latest fads are some important principles of management.

The Superboss might not need an appraisal form, but he'll give the highest priority to appraising his people. Appraisal forms were invented by Personnel to force incompetent managers to appraise their staff. The incompetent managers filled in the forms and remained incompetent. Personnel thought they had done a good job, but their contribution to profit was negative. They increased the cost of administering incompetent managers.

The Superboss sets objectives, but doesn't need forms to do it. In fact he considers setting objectives essential to his management task, as he does assessing the climate or mood of his people and their capability; not to mention, of course, the need to identify training requirements, to review careers and to brief his people.

The Superboss uses paper sparingly to support these necessary tasks of management. He's not against a simple system as long as it is sensible, efficient and helps with the job. There's nothing wrong with an appraisal form if you find it helpful. The Superboss prefers a blank sheet of paper.

ACTION TODAY

Don't let this section incite you to rebellion against all the personnel systems in the company. Don't photocopy these two pages and wave them in the face of the Personnel Manager when he or she reminds you that you are two months behind with your appraisal schedule.

Be more positive. Do the appraisals. The form filling is the least important aspect.

Look at all the other personnel systems and rather than complain about the bureaucracy ask yourself why someone thinks they're necessary. It could be that you're not doing too good a job managing your people.

ACTION NEXT MONTH

When you next come across the latest piece of jargon or some new-fangled management concept, take three steps back and examine your basic principles. Don't allow the new fashion to seduce you. Often it's just old wine in a new bottle. Keep practising your own principles rather than trying to apply what's new in people management. There isn't anything new!

REMEMBER

The system serves the SUPERBOSS, not the other way round.

Talent

One of the most exciting management tasks is talent spotting

You don't spot talent by filling in and reading appraisal forms, nor by going to Personnel and ploughing through 200 centrally-filed career potential review reports.

You don't spot talent by sitting on committees, nor by doing the work of your subordinates.

The Superboss spots talent because he notices when Lindsey Brown gives a superb presentation, or when Dan Shutze does an excellent supervisory job in an emergency, or because several customers tell him: 'That Lyn Zaleski is the best sales rep you've put on our patch for a long while. She really knows what she's talking about. She knows your product range inside out, she's service-oriented, always delivers, always keeps her word and, what's more, in her quiet efficient way is superb at handling the stroppy bastards in our office!'

The Superboss keeps an eye open for talent and excellence all the time. When he reads Rob Smith's Stage 3 latest submission the Superboss will tell himself that this guy really knows how to put together a clear succinct well presented report. He knows that he's done his homework, set out the facts well and that his recommendations are backed by an exceptionally sound business case. The Superboss will have spotted a talent.

The Superboss will create opportunities for others to show their talents. He'll organise presentations so that up and coming people can speak about their achievements, their plans, their work. The Superboss will walk the shopfloor on the lookout for potential supervisors. For the Superboss talent spotting is one of his most enjoyable pursuits at work.

ACTION TODAY

Here's some bureaucracy. Take a blank sheet of paper and write down the names of the most talented people in your department. These should be juniors who do not directly report to you.

Now write down the reasons you believe these people are so talented. Ask your immediate team to give you their list. Compare the names and then discuss the reasons for any lack of overlap.

Develop an agreed set of criteria for assessing talent.

FUTURE ACTION

Do the same thing in six months' time and compare notes. In a year's time pull out the notes and establish how many of the talented people who met your criteria have been promoted out of your department. If the answer is zero you have failed to spot and develop talent.

Now, today, go back a year and do the same thing retrospectively. What talent have you spotted and developed during these last twelve months?

REMEMBER

The SUPERBOSS has an eye for talent and develops it.

Targets

Unless you set yourself targets you will drift off course

Every day the Superboss sets himself a target to accomplish by the end of the day. He also sets himself weekly, monthly and yearly targets.

When the Superboss attends a meeting he sets himself a target to achieve during that meeting (which might be helping other people achieve their own targets).

When visiting customers the Superboss sets himself targets for the outcome even if it is merely to reinforce an important relationship.

Whatever these daily or weekly targets his most important target is to achieve the year-end results to which he is committed and which will always relate to the company's goals on profitability, customer service and people.

The Superboss also works closely with his people to help them set clear targets for what they have to achieve on a regular basis.

Whatever targets the Superboss sets he makes sure that they are challenging. The tougher the target the more stretched the Superboss and his team become and therefore the greater the probability of high performance and success.

ACTION TODAY

Make a habit of setting targets for your main activities.

When you drive to work in the morning concentrate on the targets you are going to achieve during the day and make sure they are geared to your year-end targets.

REMEMBER

The SUPERBOSS never targets a person, but always a result.

Teams

If a manager doesn't have a team, he or she can't be a manager

To be a team you have to work together.

In one company I knew, the top team were a group of individuals rather than individuals in a group. Each pursued his own individual goal, giving less than enthusiastic support to company decisions whilst following selfish sectional interests enthusiastically. The lack of cohesiveness in the top team was perceived throughout the company and had an alarmingly negative impact on the organisation climate.

The Superboss carefully builds his team. He chooses people who he knows will work well together, who will support each other, who will all identify with the same cause, the same vision and who will share the same values. Within the team the various members will use their own strengths to balance each other's weaknesses. Each member will have the opportunity to put their point of view on important decisions.

The Superboss cares for his team and spends considerable time with them. He'll brief them regularly, once a day, once a week, or once a month, depending on logistics and the type of business. He'll hold regular consultative meetings at which any team member can raise an agenda item.

He'll hold informal lunchtime sessions when they can air any topic they wish and generally chew the cud. Once or twice a year the Superboss will take his team away for a day or two, not only for an in-depth look at progress and future plans, but for some team building around the bars.

The Superboss expects and receives complete loyalty from the team. Any individual can give his or her opinion before a decision is made, but once that decision is made the Superboss expects full commitment to it. He will not tolerate anybody working against the team and would treat such 'de-commitment' by a team member as a resignation issue.

For the Superboss the team is all.

ACTION TODAY

Consult two people. First your management development specialist or a consultant, then your boss. How do they see your team functioning? Do they see it working well together? Do they see much back-biting, moaning and groaning? In their opinion is there a need for further team building? Listen carefully to what they say and compare it with your own perceptions.

ACTION NEXT WEEK

Feed back to your team the various views about how you work together, and discuss this with them. Agree ways of further developing the cohesiveness of the team.

REMEMBER

The SUPERBOSS never forgets that he is not only leader of the team, but part of it.

Thanks

It's hard to please when you receive no thanks

The Superboss *thanks* his secretary for coming in early.

The Superboss *thanks* his boss for giving him that tip-off about Mathieson's.

The Superboss *thanks* Tony Adcock for clearing out the sludge tank last night.

The Superboss *thanks* Gabriel Ramirez for raising that issue about the leaky roof.

The Superboss writes an individual note of thanks to each of the three engineers who went out in gale-force conditions over the weekend to recover the heavy goods vehicle that broke down.

The Superboss writes a note of thanks to the personnel officer who had to deal with some distraught parents when one of the company's apprentices was killed in a motorcycle accident.

The Superboss rings Sydney Owens to thank him for a superb lunch.

The Superboss writes a note of thanks to the security man who went out of his way to start his car for him.

The Superboss thanks Michele Roberts for staying late to send off some urgent mail.

The Superboss always makes a point of thanking people and of looking for opportunities to show his appreciation. People want the recognition of having done that little extra for a Superboss. They want to be thanked. The process of thanking creates a 'giving' rather than a 'taking' society where 'demands' are the order of the day.

ACTION TODAY

It is so easy to forget to thank, or not to be bothered. Thanking is not a sign of weakness. Go and give some thanks today. If you have nothing to be thankful about, then there is something seriously wrong with your department and especially you.

Starting today, pick up the phone and say 'Thanks' to anyone who put themselves out for you.

Starting today, discipline yourself to write at least one 'thank-you' note per week to someone who has made some extra effort on your behalf and the company's.

If you see nothing to thank anyone for, you must go and look for it. If you don't systematically thank people, they will systematically think you are taking them for granted. The consequences should be obvious.

REMEMBER

The SUPERBOSS expects no thanks.

Toleration

Toleration is the ability to absorb frustration, the supply of which increases with the size of the management challenge

Organisations are full of noise – people who make mistakes, who gossip, who say silly things to the boss, who act strangely. Organisations are even full of people who disagree with the boss.

The Superboss tolerates all this and much more. He absorbs a whole range of frustrations and takes action only when performance is threatened. He tolerates the eccentricities of Elvin Laker, the green-haired punk, but not when he throws a spanner in the sludge tank.

He tolerates the people who confront and disagree with him, knowing full well they could be right, even if he doesn't see it that way immediately. The Superboss tolerates the frustrations of the rumour mill, the grapevine, the gossip machines, the scandal-mongers and the 'five-second experts'. He knows that he is better off concentrating on scoring goals rather than shouting back at the crowd.

He tolerates the subordinate who humbly admits his mistake, knowing that he or she will learn from that mistake. However, the Superboss will take action when he knows the subordinate has not learnt and keeps making the same mistake. The Superboss will not tolerate adverse performance through repetitive mistakes.

ACTION TODAY

Before you go to bed tonight get find a large jar. Take it to work and label it 'Toleration Jar'.

Every time you suffer a silly frustration (your boss flicking dandruff off his collar, or the Finance Director sending you yet another instruction to economise on paper clips) make a note of it. At the end of the day, collect the notes, screw them up and throw them in the 'toleration jar'.

Take no further action unless your department's performance will clearly be affected.

At the end of the year throw a party for your staff. Unscramble the notes and use them as the basis for your speech. (Don't drink too much beforehand and don't be too personal.) Then ceremonially burn the notes without setting the company on fire.

REMEMBER

The SUPERBOSS tolerates the eccentricities of those who perform exceptionally well. He doesn't tolerate consistent low performance.

Training

You cannot train a manager unless he or she has a great thirst for learning

Managers train themselves. Without that motivation for self-improvement any attempt to train a manager will be futile.

Training courses are excellent for providing resources, knowledge, wisdom, feedback and stimulus for managers to improve themselves. But no matter how good the course or how good the instructor, a training course will do nothing for a manager unless he or she has already embarked on a life-long self-training programme.

There are some managers who complain that the company hasn't trained them. The company might well be at fault for not providing the facilities, for not encouraging training. Such companies are likely to end up with these negative moaners who complain about lack of training. The real answer is to train yourself. There is ample opportunity through self-study and self-improvement.

The Superboss encourages his supervisors and managers to be trained in the skills of leadership, management and dealing with people. The Superboss doesn't select anyone for his supervisory or managerial team who doesn't want to improve his or her skills in this area. The Superboss will stimulate the debate on managerial excellence and will encourage his team to seize every opportunity to improve. He'll search out the very best training courses and seminars for his people. He'll even call in the company training manager to help him design a supervisory and management training programme specifically geared to his own department needs.

The Superboss will jump at any opportunities to improve his own management skills. If he sees a suitable course for himself, he'll ask his boss to put him on it, if his boss hasn't thought about it first. The Superboss will seek out the best management literature to stimulate his thinking on how to improve. He'll often call together individuals or small groups to talk 'management' and to identify ways of improving. He'll encourage feedback about his own management skills so that he can learn from that.

ACTION TODAY

Call in your training manager and undertake a brief review of the training needs of the supervisors and managers in your area. Having identified the needs, ask yourself how motivated each person is to improve.

ACTION TOMORROW

Speak to each person and discuss with him or her the needs you have identified and how motivated he or she is to improve. Once agreed review your training budgets and give higher priority to arranging the required training.

ACTION NEXT YEAR

Review the success of the training.

REMEMBER

It takes a great amount of self-training to become a SUPERBOSS.

Travel

You have to go a long way to surpass travel as a motivating agent

I had great difficulty writing this section. I dedicated seven whole days in Rio de Janeiro to it and towards the end I seemed more concerned about whether my ever-deepening suntan would survive an overnight flight to London than whether I'd ever write about travel.

As I sat by the pool under the blazing Brazilian sun and watched the bronzed senhoritas sipping their caiparinhas I began to wonder why travel was such a motivator. I wandered towards the palm trees on the terrace of the Rio Palace Hotel and gazed down at the hot white sands of the Copacabana Beach curving away towards the Pão de Açúcar (Sugar Loaf) in the distance.

It was November and I knew that back in my cold rain-swept homeland a million people would give anything to be in my place.

Mind you, there would be another million miserable sods who travel a lot, say they hate it and still do as much as they can.

The Superboss knows that, for the rising junior, international travel is a great motivator. First and foremost it makes him or her feel important, it gives confidence, broadens the mind and adds excitement to a job.

The Superboss goes out of his way to create travel opportunities for his up-and-coming people. He sends them on courses in Geneva, liaison trips to Mexico City, or research projects to Hong Kong. If a person has done an exceptionally good job (mark the word 'exception' – it is not the rule), he'll even send them to Rio de Janeiro and charge it to the company.

The motivational impact of a person's first professional international travel is always great. The Superboss will use it selectively and with a high degree of discrimination. Some might say that travel is a 'jolly', but the Superboss knows that up in the Ivory Tower there are very important people who fly Concorde to New York, reserve hotel suites with jacuzzis and have meetings round the swimming pool. They call it work, but there's nothing wrong with the occasional 'jolly' either.

ACTION TODAY

Look at your travel diary for the next three months. Invite your most promising people to undertake each travel assignment on your behalf, the exception being if the destination is absolutely terrible. (I daren't suggest any – I've always loved Lagos and Sao Paulo.)

If you don't travel, and none of your team does, use your imagination and create an opportunity. Don't they produce paper clips more efficiently in Brazil?

REMEMBER

You have to travel a long way to become a SUPERBOSS.

Trust

Trust is the cornerstone of all meaningful relationships, whether at the workplace or elsewhere

The issue of trust is one of the most serious for a manager. The Superboss will always have implicit trust in his team, and his team in him.

Without trust no manager can achieve good results. In a climate of distrust organisation politics are rife, much energy is expounded protecting backs or kicking others behind theirs. Criticising everyone but yourself or the person you're talking to is an everyday occurrence. Distrust is blatantly counter-productive. The worst organisation and management relationships are generated from distrust, often derived from deep-rooted prejudices not founded at all on fact. Distrust often thrives when the reputation, the perception of the person (manager, vice-president, chief executive) is far removed from the reality.

The Superboss develops trust by devoting an immense amount of time to building honest relationships with his people. He believes in them, shows it and subsequently demonstrates that they can believe in him, trust him.

He means what he says and says what he means. The Superboss demonstrates that he is more concerned with fine action than fine words. The Superboss practises what he preaches. He develops trust by encouraging his people, rather than threatening them. If he does have to make a rare threat, then he's prepared to carry it out. He never cries 'wolf' – unless there *is* a wolf.

Absolute honesty, integrity, sincerity and compassion are the cornerstones on which the Superboss develops trust. He always gives others the benefit of the doubt, never believes 'evil' of them unless they clearly provide evidence of it. He bears neither malice nor grudges because he believes in his people, trusts them to do their very best for him and the company, as he would for them.

ACTION TODAY

Ask yourself about each member of your team. Do you completely trust him or her? If not, face the facts. Take that person aside and confront the issue. Explain why you don't think you trust him or her and then sincerely discuss ways of developing that trust.

Your second action is to find a way of surveying your team and establishing whether they trust you. Perhaps your personnel manager or a consultant could help. Explain to your team why it is so important to know and then agree with them the best way of obtaining the feedback. Don't rush at it. If there is distrust you'll make it worse by embarrassing people into saying things they don't want to say. An anonymous survey by Personnel might be the best way. But you need to follow through.

REMEMBER

You can always trust a SUPERBOSS.

Understanding people

Put yourself in the other person's shoes, then you'll understand

The Superboss always starts from where the other person is. The Superboss always puts himself in the other person's shoes.

The Superboss always asks himself: 'How would I feel if I were this person? What would I be thinking, what expectations would I have from this meeting, what anxieties might there be?'

The problems of the organisation are the problems of its people. The Superboss knows he needs to understand the people to understand these problems. He knows that the real problems are often not what people say they are. The Superboss knows that when Stuart Finch says, 'The company should do something about our dilapidated rest room', he really means, 'Our supervisor has done nothing to sort out the problem'.

The Superboss understands that others frequently project problems onto 'the Company' when the resolution lies much closer to home. The Superboss therefore tries very hard to find out what they mean when they say something. He learns to understand what motivates his people, what annoys them, what important problems they're reluctant to talk about. He learns to understand his people.

In trying to understand the Superboss will learn the true problems. He will learn from what remains unsaid, from a certain tension in the air or a sharp exchange between two people. He'll understand that some people feel inadequate in various aspects of their work, although they'll never admit it to him. Maybe they will be reluctant to submit reports (they are inadequate at writing reports) or participate in meetings (they are frightened of making presentations and speaking up). Perhaps they never go to the milling bay (they can't stand the noise).

The Superboss learns to understand his people and their problems, and because he understands he is able to help them and that helps the company.

ACTION TODAY

Think about your people. Put yourself into the shoes of the first five people you meet today. Imagine what they're thinking, what their problems are. And then, gently, unassumingly encourage them to talk about these problems. Try to understand, you'll probably learn a lot.

REMEMBER

It's easy to understand why he or she is a SUPERBOSS.

Uniqueness

The choice is yours: uniqueness or mediocrity

If you believe you are the same as everyone else you are doomed. In this increasingly competitive world customers will make choices based on what they perceive to be unique about the company's offerings. If what is on offer is the same as the competition then customer choice becomes a game of chance.

It is relatively easy to compete on product and price but what makes a company truly unique is the service it offers. To ensure that such service is innovative and consistently excellent requires teams of unique people and managers

The Superboss is preoccupied with developing uniqueness all around him. He devotes much of his daily effort to building up a unique team of people with a unique set of skills, with unique expertise and most importantly with a unique set of relationships with customers.

The Superboss recognises that Mary Green on reception is unique in knowing the names of all the company's regular customers. Furthermore she is unique in her warm and friendly welcome and the special way she helps visitors. Without Mary Green's unique contribution the company's revenue would seriously be at risk.

People like working for a Superboss because not only does he help them become unique but he makes them feel unique. He helps them develop a unique set of skills which enhances their personal worth and self-esteem. Such evident uniqueness becomes a source of pride and personal satisfaction.

ACTION TODAY

Here's your opportunity to state your 'unique selling proposition'.

Imagine you have a new Chief Executive starting Monday. He walks into your office and asks: 'What's unique about you and your team?' It's your opportunity to create a unique first impression.

What would your answer be? If it's not unique you'd better concentrate all your energies on making it so. If it's not unique you will be at risk of being assessed 'mediocre'.

REMEMBER

If there's anything unique about a SUPERBOSS it's his people!

Vacations

Executives who don't take their vacations should be jailed for two weeks

Vacations are essential. No one can do without them.

Vacations have a thousand therapeutic qualities, not the least of which is the effect on others when you're away. Vacations present a great opportunity for others to do your job – and even show they can do it better. (Can you believe that's possible?) Vacations give your secretary a chance to catch up on all that documentary diarrhoea you've left behind. Vacations enable you to prove to yourself that you are not totally indispensable. That's a salutary lesson.

The Superboss always takes his vacations because he knows that if he doesn't his team will feel guilty when they take theirs. So the Superboss sets the example and insists that his people follow.

The Superboss wants his vacation. He wants the therapy of letting some fresh air flow through his mind. He wants to sit on top of a mountain and take a long cool look at his job and work. He wants to do a little swimming and dive deeply under the surface of what's been happening these last few months. Then after the first two or three days of his vacation he wants to forget all about work. He wants to spend some time with his family who he's probably neglected these last few months.

Then, inevitably, when he begins to be bored with his week or two of vacation, he wants to go back to work, invigorated, refreshed, with (God help his people!) a thousand new ideas.

ACTION TODAY

This is the best page in the book! Take out your diary and plan your next vacation (if it's not planned already). Make sure it happens. No excuses. You must take it. No interruptions during the vacation either, unless the company's going out of business.

Next, and this should be even better, check with your immediate subordinates and make sure they have made their vacation plans. Don't all go at once. Someone might become suspicious.

REMEMBER

Vacations present the SUPERBOSS with great opportunities.

Value your people

No company is worth anything without its people – value them

Don't underestimate your people. They are a priceless part of your organisation. They are your company's most important asset. The company could not funtion if you fired them all tomorrow, nor could you replace them overnight.

The Superboss values his people. Whilst he will try to provide them with a fair and realistic level of pay he knows that you cannot price people this way. He knows that their value lies in their skills, experience and knowledge, as well as their dedication, commitment and effort. Their value is reflected in the time and effort he puts into selecting them, developing and sustaining their motivation. (Some managers spend more time choosing their car and caring for it than choosing their people and caring for them.)

Furthermore the Superboss values his people for what they are. He values their individuality, their unique contribution, the way they work together as a team. He values their opinions and views on what is going on. He values their advice, their understanding, their commitment and loyalty. He values the sacrifices they make occasionally.

The Superboss never sees his people as a simple cost on the profit and loss account. That is too simplistic a view which treats them as a disposable commodity. (Let's cut down costs. Let's cut down on people.)

The Superboss sees his people as the company's most valuable asset and this is reflected in the time and effort he devotes to protecting and developing that asset.

ACTION TODAY

Undertake a zero base analysis. Assume your immediate team all resign and leave tomorrow. Assess the time it would take to replace them and then train and develop the new appointees to the same performance level as those who have left.

Now assume *all* your people (10, 100 or 1,000) leave tomorrow. Again assess the time it would take to replace them and, furthermore, the prospects for doing so.

The conclusion should be obvious. Any one person leaving the company is a wasted asset; a waste of all the money, time and effort you and the company have invested in that person, a waste of all the expertise that the person has developed, a waste of all the valuable and loyal relationships that person has built up with customers, internal and external. Value that investment, value your people.

REMEMBER

For a SUPERBOSS to be invaluable his people must be too.

Vision

Without a clear picture of where you are going you achieve nothing

For the Superboss a vision is very personal. It is not what his organisation wants him to achieve, but what he wants to achieve himself.

It is this personal vision of success which drives him forward and it is progress towards achieving this vision which represents his main source of satisfaction.

Without vision other managers go off course and become reactive. They respond merely to the telephone, to memos, to edicts from on high, without too much thought as to where their efforts are taking them.

The vision of the Superboss is also the vision of his team. It is something they also want to achieve, something they can understand and which will also give them satisfaction if they achieve.

The vision can be short term (a dramatic reduction in customer complaints and a dramatic increase in customer satisfaction) or it can be long term (the benchmark for consistent best practice throughout the organisation).

The trouble with many organisations is that they impose objectives (or goals, or targets) on their people who then reluctantly attempt to achieve them while frequently doubting whether they can. Working with his team the Superboss creates his own challenging goals and agrees them with his bosses. These goals flow from his own personal vision for success in his own area.

What the vision cannot be is a bland set of words, as seen in mission statements all around the country. The vision is a tangible realisable picture of success. Reaching the moon is a tangible realisable vision. Winning the championship is a tangible realisable vision. Having the most highly rated department in the organisation is also tangible and realisable. Having a highly motivated team delivering service that customers consistently rate excellent is also tangible and realisable. Consistently high growth rate in terms of sales revenue and profitability is a tangible and realisable picture of success which everyone can relate to.

ACTION TODAY

Grab a sheet of paper and write down a personal vision of success for your current job. What exactly do you envisage you and your team will achieve over the next year or two – and what will give you all so much satisfaction?

ACTION NEXT MONTH

Take your team away to a pleasant country hotel and present them with your vision. Allow them to thrash it around with you and improve upon it. Conclude the day with the vision your team truly want to achieve and believe they can achieve.

REMEMBER

The SUPERBOSS is a visionary.

Walking the patch

Walking the patch is far preferable to talking in the ivory tower

The invisible manager is an impossible manager. Unfortunately, many employees think their managers are invisible. How can he see what's going on? By reading reports?

The Superboss puts the highest priority on going out and about, walking, talking, listening, learning and finding out about his people. He wanders around and finds out what they want to know, what problems they want fixed, what they enjoy about their work (he might even be able to make it more enjoyable). The Superboss shows an interest, shows he cares, shows that he wants his people to do well. He spends five minutes here and five minutes there explaining what's going on in the company while they explain to him what's happening on the job.

This cannot be achieved by issuing memos from the ivory tower, by using suggestion schemes, or producing expensive videos or sending everyone on brainwashing courses. The Superboss knows it can only be achieved by walking the patch.

The Superboss also encourages other people to walk his patch, to give him feedback. They might see things from a different perspective. He wants to learn from everyone.

A visible manager is a human manager. A visible manager walking the patch is a Superboss facing up to the everyday problems of his team. You may think that your biggest problem is next year's budget, but Colin Carey might be more concerned about his worn out lathe, or why the company cut down on apprentice recruitment this year and his son couldn't even get an interview. The Superboss needs to know, because he knows it will affect his team's motivation and performance.

Besides, the Superboss knows that walking the patch is excellent exercise!

ACTION TODAY

Set yourself a minimum standard of walking round your department at least four times a week. Your secretary should blank out half an hour or more for each of these 'walkabouts'. They should become routine, but with irregular routes, irregular times, and of varying duration (half an hour to four hours). Take note of any problems you encounter and actions you should take. Don't go behind the supervisor's back. Take him into your confidence, and obtain his co-operation. If you have more than one location, make different plans, but the principle is the same.

ACTION TOMORROW

Ask your employee relations specialist to spend a couple of hours wandering around separately, chatting to people. Then sit down together and review what he or she has found. You'll learn a great deal.

ACTION NEXT MONTH

Invite the Chief Executive to walk round your area with you. Introduce him or her to as many of your team as possible. Encourage them to say what they like. Demonstrate to the Chief Executive and to your people that you're proud of them.

REMEMBER

You shouldn't have to walk far to see a SUPERBOSS!

Writing

The ability to write is as elusive as the ability to manage

One of the distressing aspects of modern education is that students do not learn to write effectively.

The rudiments of grammar and spelling are hardly sufficient for effective written communication, resulting in reports which ramble on, unstructured, verbose and unedited. How many reports do you read which have a succinct summary, a brief introduction, a tightly written main report and clear, well presented, well substantiated conclusions and recommendations?

The Superboss doesn't report in writing unless it is absolutely necessary, but sometimes it is necessary. He doesn't produce a stream of off-the-cuff memos as a lazy substitute for face-to-face communication, but he does produce the occasional written report to his boss, his colleagues and his subordinates. It will be well researched, well presented and well written.

In his written report the Superboss will differentiate between facts and opinions, between conclusions and recommendations, between assumptions and assertions.

Writing is an important skill for management, but it is a neglected skill.

ACTION TODAY

Examine your last three written reports and severely criticise them. Analyse each report and score it out of 20 as follows (the figures in brackets indicate marks to be deducted):

Was there a clear summary?	Yes, less than $^1/_2$ page	2 marks
	Yes, more than $^1/_2$ page	(1 mark)
Was there an introduction?	Yes, less than 1 page	2 marks
	Yes, more than 1 page	(1 mark)
Did you edit it before it was sent out?	Yes, and more than $^1/_3$rd was rewritten	4 marks
	Yes, but little was changed	(2 marks)
Were there clear conclusions?	Yes, less than 1 page	4 marks
	Yes, more than 1 page	(2 marks)
Were there clear recommendations?	Yes, less than $^1/_2$ page	4 marks
	Yes, more than $^1/_2$ page	(2 marks)
Overall, was the report written in a clear, succint, easy-to-read style?	Yes, I received compliments about the report	4 marks
	Yes, but I could have polished it a little more	(2 marks)
TOTAL FOR THE PERFECT REPORT		20 MARKS

REMEMBER

What the SUPERBOSS writes must be important.

Zero in

Select your target and zero in on it

The Superboss has learnt not to be distracted by activities, problems and meetings that are not connected with his target objectives.

He zeros in on the real target and keeps his sights there, suppressing any selfish interest to pursue peripheral activities.

All his energies are concentrated on what he has to achieve and he zeros in on any problems which might stop him.

If the target is increasing production levels this month, or decreasing stock levels in the warehouse, or recruiting some hard-to-find systems programmers, or introducing a new quality control system, then he'll zero in on these targets and achieve them.

By zeroing in he focuses his team's attention on what has to be achieved. Lack of focus would dissipate their efforts.

ACTION TODAY

Zero in on the biggest problem facing you today, whether it be an employee relations, financial or output problem. Critically review your diary with your secretary and eliminate all 'flak' activity, redeploying the time to the problem you're zeroing in on.

Be careful not to eliminate time with your boss, colleagues or your staff. Their help is essential if you are to achieve your target.

But you can resign from committees which don't interest you, and postpone liaison visits which will profit you little, and cancel meetings which have no relevance to your target objectives.

Having identified the problem, having created the time, zero in and solve the problem.

REMEMBER

The SUPERBOSS zeros in on managing people successfully, for that's the only way to achieve results.

How to Make Work FUN!
An Alphabet of Possibilities ...

David Firth

With the majority of our lives spent either at work or asleep it seems crazy to consign 'fun' only to life outside of the office. Why do we leave our personalities behind when we set off for work in the morning? Why do we envy people who tell us that their work is fun, yet somehow feel laughter is out of place in the office? And how can we deliver excellent service, or be better than our competitors, if we'd rather not be working at all?

David Firth's totally irreverent book is packed with ideas for banishing boredom and bringing fun to the office. And building stronger teams and increasing productivity in the process ... Find out why you should persuade your company to train your team how to juggle, the benefits of practising saying phrases such as: "Does anyone think that I am bullshitting?", or "Does anybody here know a good joke?", seven new venues for efficient meetings, and what 'KIT' stands for, and why it's a good idea!

This book is a must for anyone who'd like to foster a team spirited positive working environment, get work into perspective (reduce stress levels), or simply enjoy work more. It should be studiously avoided by anyone who feels threatened by the very idea of deriving fun from work.

Gower

The Turbocharged Company

Igniting Your Business to Soar Ahead of the Competition

Larry Goddard and David Brown

Imagine, for a moment, that the business you own or work for is so successful that you cannot wait to get there each day. Sales are better than planned, and costs are on the decrease; the company's making money in a competitive marketplace, whilst providing exceptional value to your customers. All staff are productive and dedicated; customers write to applaud your service, not to complain.

Sounds too good to be true? But what if it could be a reality for your organization?

Goddard and Brown set out to find out how a handful of US companies stood head and shoulders above the rest. They looked at nearly 1,000 of the largest US businesses, and identified just 3% that they described as 'turbocharged' - all had outperformed their closest competitor by more than 40% over three years. All had somehow turned a level playing field into a significant competitive advantage. But how? On the face of it, they subscribed to a wide range of different business philosophies.

In this book, the authors identify the common factors - the 'turbocharged process' that put these companies out of the reach of their rivals. This total approach to business success incorporates a range of strategies such as TQM, ISO 9000, Benchmarking and Statistical Process Control (SPC), but is based on four essential foundations:

• unleashing people power
• Not just listening to, but revering your customers
• relentlessly pursuing productivity
• focusing on strengths, and on being the leader in your field.

Packed with examples from America's turbocharged companies, this book will help you build these foundations and get ahead of your competitors.

Gower